For every kid who picked up a bike...

- Dom Phipps | 2014

Matt Hoffman dismounts spectacularly over the deck of Ron Wilkerson's Lemon Grove ramp.

The 1987 AFA finals at the Velodrome in Carson, Los Angeles, Ron Wilkerson shows his all around quality in front of a watching Bob Haro.

CONTENTS

HARO

A solitary Rider casts a late afternoon shadow over the "Enchanted" Ramp in Leucadia, California. Winter of 1987.

1 | CROSSROADS

By 1988, the new sport of BMX freestyle reached its first crossroads. After five years of constant progress and innovation, the landscape had evolved into a rich, refined blend of intense neon colors and fanatical daily routines. New blood had brought new ideas to the forge, leaving both a thriving industry and a new sport in its tracks. The path to the crossroads had been energized and navigated by unconditional love for a new movement that was not only unique but also brought senses of identity and real purpose to those who understood.

The next set of trailblazers would be a younger generation––a group that had risen through local neighborhoods with keen appetites for a means of expression, an outlet for creativity that required nothing more than a bike, a fertile mind, and dedication to the cause. As the stakes got higher and the tricks followed suit, a fearless breed of teenage stars emerged with fire and passion that would both redefine the boundaries of the sport and drive it into the consciousness of their equally committed brothers around the world.

Life at 6066 Corte Del Cedro was a little different these days too. Bob Haro and Jim Ford had steered Haro into the leadership position in the thriving freestyle market, supported by a loyal team. But this dynamic began to show strain under the weight of outside forces. The crossroads was a junction crowded with familiar faces, heightened expectations, and loaded agendas. Who had the vision, confidence, and influence to lead the way forward, and what in fact did lie ahead for the new sport and its industry? By the turn of the decade, these questions would be well and truly answered....

Everything is determined, the beginning as well as the end, by forces over which we have no control. It is determined for the insect, as well as for the star. Human beings, vegetables, or cosmic dust, we all dance to a mysterious tune, intoned in the distance by an invisible piper.

- Albert Einstein

The most famous driveway in BMX leads to the "Enchanted Ramp" house in Orpheus Road, Leucadia. Complete with 2Hip Mail box.

2 FOREWORD

By Kevin Martin

In early 1989, through incredible luck and circumstance, I was handed the keys to Ron Wilkerson's Enchanted Ramp house on Orpheus Avenue in Leucadia, California. It was beyond a dream come true for a 19-year-old BMX kid from Connecticut. Ron had recently moved to a larger house nearby that was better suited to raising his young family and he wanted to rent the old house to riders, so he could come by and drop in whenever he wanted. So that spring, I became a tenant and the gatekeeper of what had become a major junction and key destination in the freestyle world.

BMX freestyle felt invincible at this point in time and the sport had quickly ballooned to its peak in popularity. Haro Bikes, which was just down the street from the house, had become the brand that set the pace within the new industry. The Enchanted Ramp was a popular destination for magazine shoots and contests throughout the late 80's, so I had some idea of what I was getting myself into when the discussion with Ron took place. And once word got out that I had the keys, the house became a clubhouse for some of the world's top BMX vert riders ––a ramp house/bed and breakfast of sorts. My good friend Rocky moved out from the east coast with me, plus Rockville BMX legend Hadji needed a place to live and skate, so he became the third original roommate.

As soon as we arrived, Rocky and I scrambled to get some crappy jobs to pay the rent,

and within a couple of days we had our first houseguests. Since Haro was so close by, some of their Midwest and east coast riders came out to Cali to avoid the harsh winter and to get some ramp riding in. Mat Hoffman, Dennis McCoy, Rick Moliterno, and Joe Gruttola all arrived with their bikes and bags to shoot a Haro magazine advert. Of course Ron W rode the ramp on a daily basis with GT's Dave Voelker, Skyway's Eddie Roman, and Scott Ewing all regular visitors. Dennis Langlais made the move West soon after I did and became another of our full-time roommates; soon after, another New England legend and close friend of mine, Joe Johnson, joined us.

When word got out that all you needed to hang out at the Enchanted Ramp was to buy a plane ticket and bring a little money for food, the phone started ringing and never stopped. The house quickly gained mythical status in the international freestyle world, and the British invasion began. Lee Reynolds and Nick Elkin pitched up about a month after we moved in and then the floodgates really opened! Over the next few years, there were never fewer than four to six Brits around the ramp on any given day. I think just about every English BMX legend passed through that house.

I learned pretty quickly that Europeans were pretty serious about "going on holiday." They would stay for a minimum of a month, and some of actually stayed for years! Mike Canning, Craig Campbell, John Yull, James

Haro's Ron Wilkerson rises into the branches of the infamous "Enchanted" Tree.

Cologne Germany 2012. L - R, Ben Snowden, Kevin Martin, Xavier Mendez, Dom Phipps (the author)

The "Enchanted" house sat directly along side the southbound I5 Freeway at Leucadia boulevard. CA.

Hudson, Jason Hassel, Andy Brown, Carlo Griggs, Effraim Catlow, Greg Guillotte, Gary Forsythe, Jason Ellis, and Zack Shaw were just some of the UK riders who "posted up" on our living room floor. In fact, so many British riders came to ride that ramp that at one point, six of them rented an apartment down the street, which we nicknamed "The British Embassy." Those years, and some of the great times we had have left me with a lifelong connection to the English people and their country.

I have never laughed so hard in my life as I did during the days I spent with those guys on the deck of that ramp. The sessions were amazing to me, having had only a quarter-pipe riding background. These guys were among the top vert riders in the sport, but sitting on the deck of that ramp on those sunny Californian days

was no different to riding with my friends back home in New Haven, and I learned quickly. We never had fewer than a couple of photo or video shoots each week on the ramp, whether it was Karl Roth and the BMX Plus! Crew coming down to shoot a bike test, or Spike, Lew, Andy or Brad McDonald shooting for Freestylin' and creating a feature on one of the guys who was staying at the house.

Next to the Enchanted ramp was a skate ramp that was two feet taller. Steve Stedham owned it and sessioned it regularly with legends including Mike McGill, Tony Hawk, and a 10-year-old phenomenon named Danny Way. After a while I came to expect anything when I woke up and walked out onto the deck of that ramp with my morning bowl of cereal. A number of time honored traditions developed throughout

these years, and most notably, when we had newcomers to the house, we would make a Tijuana run. Most of the guys were under 21 at the time, and unable to go to bars in the States, so with the exception of the ever present English guy (who had overstayed his 3-month visa), we would load up and head south. The drive back to Leucadia was a 45-mile, 4 a.m. adventure. At some point we figured out it could be done in 19 minutes—my personal theory was that if I drove with the lights off at 125 mph, I was pretty much invisible to the cops. And I was never caught, so I guess I was right! Those Tijuana tequila nights were some of the craziest nights of my life, no contest.

A typical day at the Enchanted house, even when there were no cameras or superstars hanging out, became a daily ritual of sorts. We woke and grabbed some breakfast before walking the thirty paces or so to the ramp. We sat and filled our lungs with the fresh morning air while reliving the previous night's shenanigans. A riding session usually ensued before an afternoon at the beach and a little street riding on route. Lee Reynolds took a real liking to that half pipe, and even when he broke his chain one day, rather than replace it, he just rode for weeks without one just to master pumping that ramp. His average airs were 10 feet out with huge can-can variations, and he was one of very few riders who could touch a branch from the most famous tree in BMX, which soared around 14 feet over the deck. Lee also had a habit of getting drunk and stripping naked to ride the ramp (still no chain) in the pitch black of night, He was also known to ride that ramp with his eyes closed; he mastered it in less than a year.

Ron would come down from Haro after a day of booking shows, bringing along his 1-year-old daughter, Tiffany. I remember being on the deck

Leucadia, 1989. Kevin Martin Prepares to roll in on a 1989 Haro Master.

Lee Reynolds, Kevin Martin and a friend, stuff 2Hip event Flyers into envelopes.

with him and Blyther riding, and each one of us taking turns checking on her while she sat in the baby seat. My most memorable riding day was the day I went from barely being able to do No-Footers to learning fully extended No Footers and extended No-Footed Can-Cans at my highest air. Truly, there was something magical about that ramp. I never felt as comfortable on any ramp before or after.

As great as many days were, though, there were also some very bad ones. That level of riding on that ramp created its share of victims; on several occasions we had to call the paramedics

to pick up an injured rider who had slammed and knocked himself out. We picked up broken teeth, splinted broken bones, and even once had to find a single finger that had been ripped off when a skater's ring finger caught a screw. But the darkest day at the house occurred when all of the roommates and friends, except me, went to Wichita for an AFA contest. I had to stay home because of an injury from a run-in with a few very angry surfers who had chosen to rearrange my face (literally).

As the guys started arriving back at the house from the contest, I was informed that Ron's

crash from the day before was more significant than previously known. When I had first gotten the news, I thought his injuries were no worse than any other concussion. But after I picked up some of the guys from the airport and saw the blood on Ron's helmet, I rushed over to his house and found his wife crying and saying that they didn't know if he was going to live. The next few months around the house were scary, but ended up being OK over time. Things became normal again. The incident was sobering, without a doubt; no one in the sport's hierarchy had been injured that severely before.

Brian Blyther was a regular visitor, and a master of the enchanted ramp transition.

Kevin Martin ran West coast distribution for a the Trend Bike Source, out of Texas for a period. Pictured here working from the "Office" of the second Enchanted house in La Costa, CA.

The Russian Ice breaker. Hanging with the best riders in the world will bring out the best in your vert skills. Kevin Martin stretches a no Footed Can - Can.

Another noteworthy day at the house was when we walked out to the ramp and found some German ramp rider sitting on the deck with a bike and a large backpack. He explained that he had travelled from Germany to ride the Enchanted ramp, but even more amazing was the fact that with his pack, he had ridden the 30 miles to the house from the San Diego airport. He asked to camp in the yard but we decided that his story was worthy of a spot on the living-room floor.

At the time we were all pretty broke and had to rely on anyone with a car to do anything. One of my buddies from my movie-theater job liked to shoot photos and had the nicest car of anyone we knew, so he was our go-to guy; I remember stuffing five us in his VW Rabbit to go get groceries or do laundry. Matt Sully-Sull is still one of my closest friends. As for the house, at its most crowded I counted 14 people sleeping on the floor. During my time there, street riding (adapted from skateboarding) became pretty popular; I recall regular trips to downtown San Diego to ride with Pete Augustin and the rest of the Dirt Brothers crew.

Of course Voelker, Eddie Roman, Sean Yaroll, and Chris Day were usually in attendance at any downtown session. I saw the birth of that niche within BMX freestyle as I witnessed those legends master wall rides and handrails. On one of Mat Hoffman's visits I watched him do one of the first rail slides ever attempted, down a 15-plus-step staircase! Not only had this never been done before, it had not even been imagined. I also rode flatland at the beach from time to time. Rocky was really amazing and Hammels locals, including Henry "Hank" Davis and Haro rider Dave Nourie, made days at Mission Beach really fun.

Soon after moving to the house I started working at 2Hip and as an announcer for Haro from time to time, and so became close friends with Bob Haro and Bill Hawkins. Regular trips to Haro became routine, and of course any bikers visiting the company hung out at the Enchanted house while Bob and Bill were busy running the business. Those were truly golden days: while the scene at the ramp house was unfolding, Haro Bikes was skyrocketing.

In Carlsbad, Bob was surrounded by a growing collective of characters who helped the company not only continue to set the pace of the sport but also to lead the way. An average day at the office involved laughter, Mexican food, road-trip preparation, visitors of every kind, product development, product testing, and the general collecting of swag. Day-to-day participants included accountants, marketing gurus, project managers, team managers, photographers, relatives, and the best riders in the sport. The atmosphere in Carlsbad was exciting, relaxed, and fun, and it cultivated innovation with a perfect blend of some of the most creative, talented minds and athletes at the top of their game.

As the sport grew to its zenith - an estimated 20+ million riders - it became apparent that not only was BMX freestyle firmly established, it was actually a legitimate sport with a huge associated industry. Anyone who took off on this perfect BMX freestyle wave was having the ride of their lives. Bob Haro's vision had become a reality beyond his wildest dreams.

Bob Haro holds court during the filming of the "Team Haro" video in 1988.

3 | LOOK BACK

The television screen projects a grainy-but-familiar image, first seen more than a decade earlier. Astronaut Neil Armstrong, clad in a bulky space suit, stands next to a planted flag in a barren lunar landscape known only as the Sea of Tranquility. The flickering flag brings a burst of neon color to an otherwise monotone image, while the voice of John Lack intones over a thrashing guitar: "Ladies and Gentleman, Rock and Roll." On August 1, 1981, at 12:01 am EDT, the MTV Generation was born, and global youth culture stood at the dawn of a new era.

Some thousands of miles away, in the sprawling San Fernando Valley, a second-unit film crew is setting up a bicycle chase for an ambitious new movie, A Boy's Life. This sequence, filmed with the aid of Bob Haro and a group of local BMX racers, will become the catalyst for a surge in demand that will propel the twenty-inch bicycle into a whole new world. By the end of the year, the film will have a new title: E.T. the Extra-Terrestrial.

Ron Wilkerson and Brian Blyther pose for the 1986 Haro product catalogue.

The early 1980s was a period of accelerated growth and progress for the new sport of freestyle BMX. By the middle of the decade, the future of both the sport and its burgeoning industry looked assured. As participation in racing and freestyle increased, a steady flow of talented new riders emerged from towns and cities across a vast geographical region of the United States and beyond. With this uplift in demand came a raft of untapped opportunities. As a result, a group of ambitious young brands began to eagerly harvest the spoils of the explosive imposition, as fanatical riding scenes quickly emerged in the Midwest and South, and along the East Coast.

By the end of 1984, most of the interested parties had witnessed the mind-blowing AFA King of the Skate Parks––a contest series centered around two Southern California skate parks, in Upland and Del Mar. Having quickly recognized the steep increase of skill and ability among a new generation of riders, the event facilitators–AFA President Bob Morales and Don Hoffman, the son of the Upland Park owners–had also begun to use their resources to bring the series as much exposure as possible. The quality and accessibility of the events, in particular the duels between GT's Eddie Fiola and Haro's Mike Dominguez, not only made compelling viewing but also fueled a friendly business rivalry between the two brands. As this rivalry began to gather momentum in the press, the series inspired a vast amount of imagery in old and new media. Soon after the early rounds of the 1984 contest series, work was underway at Wizard Publications to launch the first dedicated freestyle 'zine––an inspired moment that instantly legitimized the sport to the eyes of the watching world. The resultant publication, FREESTYLIN', energized the scene and created a fanatical community around the new sport.

Steve Cassap became the first Australian freestyle rider to gain sponsorship from Bob Haro in 1984.

Early 1985 at the AFA Freestyle contest in Pleasanton, Northern California.
Haro's Tony Murray clicks a text book "look back" for the cameras.

The "Morning Session", Boblingen, Stuttgart, Germany, 1987. L-, PTR Team riders Rainer Strecker and Patrick, Haro's Ron Wilkerson, Thomas Rank (PTR), Stephan Prantl, Michael, Bernd Schneider, Brian Blyther and Dave Nourie. Ron Wilkerson rode for the entire session without a chain and blasted his entire repertoire of tricks.

Friendly rivalries played out between rival brand's Haro and GT throughout the early 1980's. This custom "Number 1" GT cake, was a gift to Haro from Gary Turner, following Eddie Fiola victory in the 1984 King of the Skate Park Finals. The cake was quickly "remodeled" by Jim Ford, and sent back to the GT Offices in Huntington Beach.

Another driving force behind the unparalleled growth in freestyle was a tried-and-tested formula that presented the very best of the sport while also nurturing and radicalizing its impulsive, youthful audience. The old-fashioned "rubber to the road" method of promotion held nothing back. As early as 1981, when freestyle was still little more than a novelty in comparison to the established BMX race scene, Bob Haro had recognized that the only realistic way to project the message and grow interest in the sport was to take the show to the audience. Factory freestyle tours represented a major commitment for the bike companies and their riders, both personally and financially, but the events also drew consumers and the trade together. Typically, a tour would weave a route from the West Coast to the East Coast, deviating occasionally to areas of high interest in the northern U.S. and Canada and dropping anchor in the highly populated Midwest.

With most factory freestyle brands under the leadership of young entrepreneurial characters like Bob Haro, this exuberant physical presence in the market won hearts and minds and created passionate new advocates.

Across the Atlantic, 7000 miles away from the beaches and boulevards of Southern California, a parallel BMX universe was unfolding. An uprising in the UK in the early '80s had evolved similarly to the U.S. scene, with a boom in BMX racing preceding the introduction and subsequent diversion of freestyle. Here, as in the U.S., Bob Haro saw the opportunity early and positioned his brand instinctively and intelligently despite limited resources. Forays onto the continent were also encouraging, as a similar passion for the sport sprouted in disconnected and remote regions of Europe. A short visit to Australia, to ride freestyle demos at a motocross event, affirmed

the genuine opportunities that lay ahead for the brand: on his return to the U.S. in late 1983, Haro had a new haircut and a full order book.

The expansion of the AFA Masters series in the mid-1980's also boosted participation levels in the sport. Affiliated local contest's, in new and untapped regions of the United States served as a development system for committed, local, riders, some of whom would go on to become national freestyle icons

As the decade reached its midpoint, all was well at Haro HQ in Carlsbad. The freestyle world had become a prosperous place, and those at Haro could feel justified in considering the company the leading force in the young industry. But despite this position of strength, things were about to change at Haro Designs in more ways than one...

Brian Blyther and the UK rider Craig Campbell pose in front of the hallowed Pipeline Skate Park in Upland, CA. Campbell was in town to ride in the 1985 King of the Skate Parks finals where he placed third in the pro class.

Brian Blyther, Ron Wilkerson and Bob Haro pose for a photograph in downtown San Diego during the filming of the 1988 "Team Haro" promotional video.

4 | NEW HORIZONS

With the founding of West Coast Cycle Supply in the 1950s, Leo and RosaBelle Cohen created the first truly national bicycle, and accessory Distribution Company in the United States. The business operated from a modest location in down town Los Angeles, before relocating to a trade park in Carson years later. As the 1960s began, RosaBelle Cohen came to realize that to realistically grow the West Coast business and turn the tide of dissatisfaction that was brewing in the domestic trade due to inferior-quality bicycle imports from Europe, the company needed a unique and more-efficient supply chain. After the retirement of his parents, 23-year-old Howie Cohen became the new company president in 1963. When the West Coast buyers began to look beyond the United States for suppliers, Howie was soon dispatched on a research visit to Japan to assess the feasibility of working directly with the expanding Asian bicycle industry.

After a six-week period of due diligence, Howie identified the Kawamura Sangyo bicycle factory as a potential trade partner. Kawamura had been producing and exporting a range of affordable adult bikes to the US for only a short time, so the two parties were quickly able to reach an agreement to collaborate on increasing export/import volume and profitability in ways that would utilize West Coast Cycle's distribution network of domestic bicycle dealers. Their first joint venture, promotion of the American Eagle brand, was so successful that West Coast was able to sustain steady growth into the early 1970s. By 1974, however, having built a much more extensive portfolio of Japanese brands and factories, Howie Cohen opted to sell his shares in West Coast and start a new California-based distribution venture that he named Everything Bicycles. Throughout the 1970s and 1980s, Howie continued to network

The Interbike trade show in Long Beach, CA, 1988.

Brian Blyther "Fence plant's" under lights at the Pipeline in late 1988. The park would be closed and demolished within a year of this photograph being taken.

and trade with the growing Asian bicycle industry; in 1980, he played a key role in Steven Spielberg's choice of the Kuwahara BMX bike for the iconic chase scene in his blockbuster, E.T. the Extraterrestrial. This beloved bicycle industry pioneer and legend passed on in 2013.

In the fall of 1986, Sid Dunofsky, president of the West Coast Cycle Distribution Company, arrived at the Haro premises in Carlsbad with an ambitious proposition. Since the conception and release of the Haro Freestyler, the very first dedicated freestyle frame-and-fork combination; Haro had become almost untouchable in the developing freestyle market. Each year beyond that pivotal moment in the summer of 1982, the company had chalked up another round of

spectacular growth. In addition, the success of the Freestyler had led to concepts that were even more ambitious. By the mid-1980s, the Haro product line included a series of three dedicated freestyle bikes, each available in multiple color combinations and aimed at a different style of riding. The company was also leading the way in the after-market parts and accessories business, and would cement its claim to the most advanced product line in the BMX market within the year by launching a stylish and well-designed collection of dedicated BMX clothing.

Dunofsky wasted no time making his intentions clear: he wanted to buy Haro and absorb it into his thriving brand portfolio at West Coast Cycle. Preferring to retain Bob Haro and Jim Ford in

senior operational roles, he offered increased financial resources that would enable them to scale up and completely dominate the BMX market through the later decade and beyond. But BMX wasn't the only thing on Dunofsky's agenda. He also saw opportunities to establish an advanced Haro mountain-bike range––an ambitious plan, considering the competition from a group of innovative mountain-bike brands including Specialized, Gary Fisher, and Breezer as well as Haro's arch-BMX rival GT, which was already diverting significant resources to the larger-wheel category.

Surprised but not at all unwilling to consider the buyout, Haro and Ford took a meeting with their accountant. Neither had seriously considered such an acquisition, although it was known that Bob Haro was becoming disillusioned with the operational responsibilities that had accompanied the company's rapid growth and regularly drew him away from his accustomed place at the design table. In light of Dunofsky's offer, and the security of a five-year executive contract with full benefits, Bob Haro entered into negotiations for the sale of Haro Designs. By early 1987 the company had new owners–– and a new destiny.

In the spring of 1987, in a bid to raise knowledge and awareness of BMX among West Coast Cycles staff, star Haro riders Dennis McCoy and Ron Wilkerson were dispatched to Los Angeles to perform a freestyle show in the company warehouse. The new owners' domain included a sizeable infrastructure as well as a range of products that covered numerous categories within the wider bicycle market. With the acquisition of Haro Designs, they had gained immediate credibility within the vibrant BMX freestyle scene. In addition, a lesser-known benefit would also continue to develop through the rest of the decade.

In the spring of 1985, pro BMX Racer Pete Loncarevich was expected at the Haro offices in Carlsbad for his annual co-sponsorship discussion. Haro had maintained a worthy presence within the International BMX racing scene, largely via the number-plate lines, accessories, and clothing, and of course the presence of the affable Ron Haro on the circuit as manager of sponsorship and teams. Loncarevich arrived prepared for the meeting (which he considered a formality that included a welcome opportunity to look at new gloves, plates, and race leathers), but it soon become obvious that Haro and Ford had a more ambitious agenda in mind. Their proposal

included an exciting prospect: the formation of the Haro Racing Division, and a new position for Loncarevich as consultant on the geometry of the bike that he would ride in competition. After a lengthy contract dispute with his sponsor CW, Loncarevich officially began to compete exclusively for Haro in April of 1986; by the end of the spring 1987 season, he had won almost every title and accolade worth mentioning on the new Haro RS1 Race BMX he had helped to design.

The buyout and new line launch were creating the usual accounting and operational headaches for the back-room staff at both companies. In the boardroom, however, the "new" Haro Designs was being positioned to make its most ambitious assault yet on the BMX market. With its manufacturing resources in Taiwan both established and productive, Haro and Ford wanted to quickly expand the product lines into market areas that had previously been off-limits. The demise of Torker (Haro's early manufacturing partner, based in Orange County, California) had forced Jim Ford to re-appraise suppliers; by late 1983 he had begun to negotiate a productive relationship with two Taiwanese brothers, Sam and Alan Wong, via a US-based trading company called Teel Technologies. The Wong's owned and managed two dedicated bicycle manufacturing and assembly plants in the Taichung district of Taiwan, called Anlen and Anlun industries. From the earliest days of this new relationship, collaboration between Haro and the brothers had gone from strength to strength. Both parties worked closely with the same objectives: continuous innovation of market-leading products and ambitious but realistic growth targets. Teel, which became the catalyst for management and oversight, extended a line of

credit to Haro based on the latter's forecast of future business.

Beyond the industry boardrooms and private bathrooms, however, the riders were beginning to exert their own influence on the direction of the sport. Not only was the AFA Masters Series peaking in popularity, with record attendances recorded at the New York contest in 1986, no fewer than six contests were staged that year in major cities across the United States. A relatively new pro class rider, Haro's Dennis McCoy, would dominate the 1987 series and, in the process, begin to directly influence the direction of flatland riding with his spectacular fast-linked runs that were packed with advanced and sometimes incomprehensible tricks. A professional rivalry began to develop among the regular contenders in the pro flatland ranks. Veteran RL Osborne, up-and-coming GT Rider Martin Aparijo, and Haro's McCoy spent the 1987 season competing at a level of skill and intensity that rendered them virtually untouchable: the three traded among the top three positions at contests throughout the year. McCoy, however, was also a contender in the Pro Ramp class, and by the end of the year had completed his dominance by winning the AFA Pro overall title in only his second full year as a professional freestyle rider.

Away from the AFA Series, innovation and progress within the vert-riding scene were also in full swing. Haro pro Ron Wilkerson firmly believed that the future of "vert" lay with the introduction of dedicated half-pipe contests. The current AFA Masters format revolved around two 6-foot quarter-pipes, stationed at either end of the contest arena; in the opinion of a number of pro riders, this arrangement no longer reflected the style of riding that was happening beyond the contest scene.

Bob Haro and Bill Hawkins pose in front of racks of neon Haro Sport, Master and FST frames at the Anlen factory in Taichung.

Pistol Pete Loncarevich leads the way for the newly created Haro Racing Division at the Murray World Cup in Dixieland, 1986.

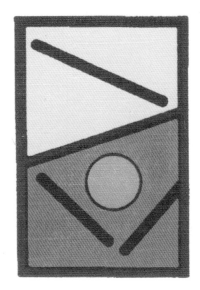

King of Vert

A new era begins. L - R - Ron Wilkerson, Jim Ford (Haro VP), Bill Hawkins (Freestyle Team Manager) and Dennis McCoy. McCoy and Wilkerson visit the West Coast Cycle facility to demonstrate freestyle for Haro's new owners and staff at WCC in Carson, Los Angles - Early 1987.

Riding half-pipes demanded stamina, fast thinking, and smooth style; the desired results were bigger air and a more-inventive approach to dropping in and riding. Wilkerson and his young family had been living in North County, San Diego since late 1984, when he had joined Haro as a professional rider and team manager from rival brand GT. In February of 1986, he purchased a house on Orpheus Road, in Leucadia, and the legend of the Enchanted Ramp House began. Within weeks of moving in, Ron started building in a large plot adjacent to his family home.

The Enchanted house quickly became a key destination for many US-based freestyle riders. As the half-pipe format began to re-energize the

scene, a community of established pros and new young riders began to take vert riding beyond previously imagined goals and boundaries. In the closing months of 1986, Wilkerson stepped up with an ambitious vision: a contest series based around the new format. Drawing on the vast network of friends and connections he had built around the country through years of constant touring and traveling, he began to look for a suitable venue to stage the debut 2Hip King of Vert half-pipe contest. Minnesota locals Rich Hansen and Kurt Schmidt were among a group of trusted friends who convinced Ron to stage the event in their state, where a sizeable and passionate BMX freestyle community had grown through the early 1980s. A suitable venue was found in Eden Prairie, at an indoor skate park named Ramp City and owned by two local

riders, Marty Schlesinger and Charlie Kasbohn. In a last-minute twist of fate, however, problems with the park's insurance coverage forced Ramp City to close. Luckily, the ramp was relocated to a vacant barn in the nearby town of Lesueur, and after some hasty modifications that involved removing part of the ramp to ensure it would fit between the rafters of the barn, the contest went ahead as planned.

The 2Hip King of Vert contest series was a pivotal moment in the evolution of freestyle BMX in the late 1980s. The success of the debut contest in Minnesota, and the ongoing support of sponsors that included Haro Designs and Vision Streetwear gave rise to a second event. The Enchanted Ramp Jam, held on December 13

The pros were all riding half-pipes away from the contests and the AFA decided they wanted to continue with quarter-pipes and kick-turn ramps. Everybody had half-pipes: I had one and Mike D had one and that's what we were riding. Around the beginning of 1986, I approached Bob Morales and said, 'Let's do a half-pipe series. I'll run it for you and you can call it the AFA Series.' By this time Bob was no longer a rider and was more of a businessman. I was a rider, and I knew what we were all doing as riders, and where the contest scene needed to go. The half-pipe scene was driving the level of progression in vert riding, and that motivated me to create an alternative to the AFA format.

– Ron Wilkerson

Brian Blyther "X'd Up" at the 2Hip King of Vert Finals in Leucadia in 1987.

L - R Brian Blyther, Rick Moliterno and Ron Wilkerson prepare to shoot a scene for the Team Haro 1988 video, in Downtown San Diego.

Rick Moliterno rides the 2Hip Meet the Street blocks and launch ramp at the Enchanted house in Leucadia.

We bought the house because it had a big open area for a ramp. It was by the freeway, which worked because ramps make noise and there would maybe be less neighborhood problems. The ramp was super-solid—the perfect ramp of the time. I looked at all of the different ramp plans that I could find, from local skaters I knew, and plans published in magazines, and just morphed all of the best bits into one half-pipe. It took a couple of full-on weeks to build it, and anybody who was around at the time helped out. The experience of building a ramp is so satisfying, it's like nothing else; it's almost as good as riding it. As it comes together you start getting excited to ride it. If you can build a ramp, you can build anything. As soon as you get a layer of plywood on—it's on. Then you build it up.

I called up Jim Ford at Haro, and all of my sponsors, and got them each to pitch in some money. Back in those days it wasn't much, but it was enough to make it happen. Of course the sponsors liked what we were doing because we knew so many people across the country, and word got out there really fast. We put the banners up and the first event was in Minnesota, an area where we had a lot of friends who could help to make it happen. Somebody knew somebody who had a half-pipe and we had to set it up in a barn after the original venue closed down. This was in November and I was like, 'OK then, let's do it.' The event was during the first snow of the year and it was literally freezing. There was like four to six hundred people, I don't remember exactly—but it was a lot. The energy at that event was electric, it was the best of what we were doing away from the mainstream contests and everybody was so psyched. We decided on a jam-style format, and everybody was pushing and supporting each other. It was the first time that riders were up on the deck throughout the entire contest. Somebody would do something rad in their run, and it would make you psyched to do something rad in yours. Everybody was yelling for each other. It was like the dawning of a new era.

– Ron Wilkerson

hosted in the grounds of Wilkerson's home in Leucadia. There was now a genuine alternative to the AFA Masters Series. In fact, as the decade unfolded, the King of Vert Series would replace the Masters to become the premier event in the vert scene.

By the mid-1980s, virtually every established BMX brand had recruited a team of factory riders. These were a mixture of paid and contracted professionals, along with a group of younger amateur riders who acted as understudies and were paid with products and traveling funds from the brand they represented. Haro Designs, which began dispatching teams to distant regions of the United States, Europe, and even Asia in 1984, was well aware that this formula was the very best way to reach and influence the mass market. Each January, the first calendar consideration for just about every interested party in the freestyle industry was the summer months, when schools were out of session. In fact, touring became such a high priority for the freestyle brands that almost every sponsor's commitments throughout the year were scheduled around June, July, and August, when its team would leave California in a truck, a fold-down ramp in tow and, clutching a list of dates and destinations, to embark on a cross-country crusade based on a network of local bicycle shops. In 1986, Haro demonstrated its confidence in this formula by sending out two separate teams for the whole summer. Senior riders Dave Nourie, Ron Wilkerson, and Brian Blyther headed overseas to Europe and Japan while Dennis McCoy, Tony Murray, and Rich Sigur criss-crossed the United States. The summer of 1987 saw a similar arrangement; however, the demand for Haro tour shows within the United States was so immense that both teams set out in early June to cover almost 120 individual show commitments on what was titled

Bill Hawkins, Jim Ford and Ron Haro enjoy some downtime in the shadow of Haro's new RS Group 1 Race frames. Corte Del Cedro, Carlsbad.

The Haro Rampage Tour. The tried-and-tested trio of Wilkerson, Blyther, and Nourie headed out of California with a local surfer named Nar announcing, while the newly formed team of Dennis McCoy, Joe Johnson, and Rick Moliterno set off in a different direction with Australian Nick Jonze on the mic.

The year 1987 would prove to be the most successful and lucrative in the early history of Haro Designs. In its first year of new ownership, the company made its intentions and ambitions clear by doubling its orders of complete bikes from 22,000 units to 45,000 and by expanding its ranges into new categories, including the specialist mountain-bike market. The company's top line was in excellent shape and Sid Dunofsky was beginning to look like a genius. But could this streak continue?

April - 1987. Haro's Joe Johnson destroys the amateur class at the Houston King of Vert contest.

East coaster; Paul DeLaiarro represented Haro in contests and freestyle deomo's in a variety of countries during the mid to late 1980's. Here, observed by Brian Blyther, he prepares to demonstrate a trick he invented - The cherry picker drop in.

Paul Delaiarro riding a first generation Haro Master at the Les Bowles AFA contest in Abington, Massachusetts In 1984. Delaiarro broke into Bill Curtin's Haro East coast sponsored "Freestyle Force" team a few weeks before this contest.

5 | EAST COAST

Bob Haro and Bob Morales were under no illusions as they rolled out of the Haro premises in Torrance in the summer of 1981. Opportunities to travel and experience the diversity of the country were limited for many American kids, and this trip was more significant than most. Ultimately, its magnitude would be defined by the age, experience, and ambition of the crew on board: the two Bobs, plus Haro's younger brother Ron.

This, the first official BMX freestyle tour of its kind, would take the trio of born-and-bred Californians into new environments and unfamiliar cultures. Nonetheless, the goals remained the same: to energize the youth of the country, and to establish Haro Designs as the driving force and cutting-edge brand behind a creative new sport that was called, simply, "freestyle."

An important segment of the tour would take the newly formed team to a number of key East Coast destinations. BMX racing had become popular in most major U.S. towns and cities since its arrival in the late 1970s; on the East Coast, the scene had been legitimized by the formation of the National Bicycle League, a governing body founded in 1975 by motorcycle racing promoter George Esser. By the early 1980s, racing had evolved into a highly regulated and competitive sport. Thus the arrival of freestyle––a new, raw, creative alternative to BMX racing––represented both good fortune and perfect timing.

BMX Action magazine now began to include specific coverage of freestyle, with frame-by-frame tutorials on how to perform certain tricks and even plans and guidance for building trick ramps. Before long, small neighborhood teams were forming in towns and cities up and down the East Coast, hauling ramps into arenas at BMX races, and showcasing freestyle to captivated audiences. This momentum would be augmented by the arrival of the creator of the sport, in a Dodge truck, with his equally entrepreneurial teammate and equally passionate younger brother.

By the time the Haro Team rolled into the Commonwealth Pier Exhibition Hall in Boston, late in the summer of 1981, demand for a close look at what the rising stars of the sport were able to do had reached a fever pitch. In the audience that day were Bill Curtin and Paul Delaiarro, two young local freestylers who would play significant roles in promoting and creating a stronghold for Haro on the East Coast through the mid-1980s. Curtin was part of a fledgling but highly active local team, Cruze Brothers, whereas Delaiarro––the younger of the two–– spent most of his free time trying to catch Bill's attention.

Curtin knew he would have a few opportunities to make a case for direct support from Haro, having managed to acquire passes to the trade show from a local bike dealer. His moment

I did everything in my power to impress Bill Curtain so he would give me a spot on the team. I was all over it.

– Paul Delaiarro

arrived as he helped the team build ramps for the demonstration. The vision Curtin pitched to Bob Haro involved an exclusive Haro nursery system, just on the East Coast, that would develop riders for the brand. Haro showed interest, but because he and Morales still had roughly 10,000 miles to cover that summer, he and Curtin agreed to talk again when Bob was back in California.

Meanwhile, in Baltimore, Maryland, two teenage brothers became absorbed into the lifestyle through magazine coverage and word of mouth. Summer break in 1983 was spent dirt jumping, which quickly led to the construction of wooden ramps and long daily riding sessions with friends. Both Joe and Jeremy Alder would go on to represent Haro Designs at the national contest level after progressing through the NFA contest series as regional champions.

The call finally came for Bill Curtin in late 1983, courtesy of a Boston bike shop that provided his telephone number after a chance call from Bob Haro, who was attempting to track him down to reopen discussions about Haro East Coast. Two weeks later, boxes of Haro frames, Skyway wheels, and uniforms, as well as Am'e grips and Vans shoes were unloaded in front of Curtin's house while his friends looked on in amazement. That group included Paul Delaiarro, who had convinced Curtin to sign him up and now proudly owned a genuine Haro jersey with his name across the shoulders.

Bill Curtin connected with Bob Haro at Commonwealth Pier exhibition Hall, in Boston, during the Summer of 1981 to discuss his vision for a Haro nursery system on the East Coast.

Back in New England, in his parents' back yard, another young racer-turned-freestyler was honing his carpentry skills in hopes of catching some serious air. The series of ramps developed by Joe Johnson, along with a group of equally possessed friends, was becoming more ambitious by the week. This back-yard freestyle laboratory became the perfect finishing school for Johnson; by 1985, after impressive runs at a number of local contests, he had inked a factory deal with Haro.

Flash forward to Chittenango, New York, in 1987, where a 12-year-old aspiring flatland rider named Dave Mirra is about to make a phenomenal rise to fame. His break comes after he attends a Haro tour show in Liverpool, New York, where he catches the eye of pro rider and team manager Ron Wilkerson. Circumstances will ultimately interrupt his association with the Haro brand, but over the next decade––during the peak of the X Games era––Mirra will become one of the biggest names in freestyle history while riding for Haro Designs.

Haro's dominance of the freestyle scene now looked secure. But another challenge was looming large in the New England freestyle scene: the Californian BMX brand GT, Haro's closest rival in the freestyle market. In 1984, a hard-fought King of the Skate Parks series in Southern California during the AFA contest season threw the two brands together in a head-to-head pro division match-up. Haro's Mike Dominguez beat GT's Eddie Fiola in the finals, even though both riders missed a round due to injury or overseas tour commitments. This series seemed to crystalize the rivalry in the eyes of the BMX press, so it was no surprise when the same dynamic began to develop on the East Coast.

GT's Eddie Fiola spent the summer of 1984 promoting the brand at European tour events. The final leg of the tour brought Fiola back to the U.S. East Coast to ride a series of shows at National Guard armories and to judge some local amateur contests. During these shows he met former schoolteacher and contest organizer Ron Stebenne, who formed the Mountain Dew GT Trick team soon after. The presence of both Haro and GT within the local contest scene, and the pressure and intensity of the rivalry that began to develop, would drive the riders' progression and skill levels to new heights.

Eventually, the freestyle riding scenes that were also percolating in New York, New Jersey, Pennsylvania, West Virginia, North and South Carolina, Baltimore and Florida became so widespread that in 1985 the National Freestyle Association was formed. Richard Hutchins, owner of the Hutch Hi- Performance BMX brand, founded this dedicated East Coast contest organization that was designed to drive freestyle participation in the region. The next year, however, the association was sold to the United States Bicycle Association; in turn, the larger organization was absorbed into the American Bicycle Association later that year.

These years of continuous growth and local promotion in the East Coast freestyle scene reached a pivotal moment as the 1985 contest season drew to a close in December. The American Freestyle Association had decided to stage its Masters Finals in Manchester, New Hampshire—a high-profile event that gave East Coasters an important opportunity to compete alongside the established Californians. Although Haro's Ron Wilkerson won the Overall Pro title, capping a year of total dominance in both the U.S. and Europe, the similarities of skill and ability

Joe Johnson stretches a tabled no-footed can-can in his mothers yard in Stoughton, Massachusetts, 1987.

between the riders from opposite sides of the U.S. could not be denied. From now on, new events––including the 2Hip King of Vert half-pipe series––would have a regular presence on the East Coast. At last, freestyle had become a truly national sport.

Brian Blyther - Washington DC King of vert. 1987

Fridley, MN, 1983. Dale Matson's "Open Air Trick Team" demos for the growing local freestyle fan base.

6 | HEARTLAND

With the exception of the West Coast, no region of the United States could lay claim to such an influential and progressive early BMX scene as the highly populated Midwest. In the 1970s a collection of 12 states, including Illinois and Missouri, and cities in the region including Minneapolis, Detroit, and Chicago (the country's third-largest city), became a stronghold for the developing BMX racing scene. As the decade turned, and the freestyle scene exploded out of the beach towns of the West Coast, the Midwest saw no shortage of energy and anticipation for the new freestyle movement. As exposure for the new sport grew and the decade began to unfold, a period of enterprising but organized chaos ensued.

As the introduction of racing to the Midwest nurtured a new skill among the young, kids with BMX bikes were busy experimenting with dirt jumps and homemade ramps. Any obstacle that represented the potential to get air was identified and utilized until it was worn out, replaced with a new and improved version, or declared off-limits. The timely entrance of freestyle to the region arrived in 1981 with the revered BMX Action and Haro trick teams out of California.

Dale Matson, a competitive BMX racer and freestyler from Coon Rapids, Minnesota, became a key figure in the Midwest freestyle scene in the 1980s. Along with his friend Kurt Schmidt, Dale set out on a mission to promote the sport through a series of locally organized freestyle shows. Later in the decade, he became the nucleus for the growing community of local freestyle riders when he conceived and

Kansas City's prodigy ,and future Haro pro Dennis McCoy, takes it to the street on his Hutch Race bike

My first glimpse of freestyle was RL Osborne and Mike Buff with their BMX Action Trick Team coming to Minnesota, wearing their star-studded uniforms. I will never forget Mike Buff asking for 15 volunteers to lie down so he could jump over the lot of us. I was Number 15 in that line, and I still remember Buff jumping over all of us and nearly landing on me! After that show, I forgot all about BMX racing and started practicing the tricks I had seen. Pretty soon you would see makeshift quarter-pipes and half-pipes built up in people's back yards, empty suburban lots, and in the streets.

– Dale Matson

Supporting the Pro Haro USA Team at a tour show held at Penn Cycles, MN. Dale Matson with Kurt Schmidt, Billy Anderson, Scott Anderson, Alden Frostad and Chris Schorn facilitated the Midwest Freestyle Series, better known as the MFS. He also became a key figure in the regional expansion of the American Freestyle Association.

A local scene quickly developed and became a catalyst for new connections and friendships. Energized by the challenge, sporadic groups of like-minded kids were patrolling local neighborhoods; picking up new, equally obsessed friends; and joining up to form freestyle crews. For many, freestyle represented youthful liberation––an opportunity to break out and express untapped creativity––and, in some cases, a first taste of true independence. The seeds had been sown, and similar scenarios soon sprang up across the Midwest in the tracks of the early freestyle tours.

The influence of certain local riders was undoubtedly responsible for the momentum and direction of the thriving neighborhood freestyle scenes. In Kansas City, Missouri, future Haro rider Dennis McCoy and his friend Shawn Dixon formed a freestyle crew that became known throughout the city as the BMX Brigade. McCoy and Dixon energized the local scene as the brigade quickly swelled in numbers. During a typical week, the fanatical crew would set out on all-night riding sessions. The brigade quickly gained mythical status among riders throughout Kansas City as the scene zoomed up a steep nightly curve of progression and (harmless) hell-raising.

The scene began to produce mythical stories and new names. Iowa's Rick Moliterno, Kansas City's Rick Thorne, and Minnesota's Kurt Schmidt and Marty Schlesinger all paid their dues and transcended their local scenes to become paid factory-freestyle riders. In Ohio,

a former synchronized swimmer and junior Olympian named Kris Dauchy became the first factory-sponsored female rider in the United States, having turned to the new sport when she developed an allergy to chlorine. When Dale Matson decided that the time was right to capitalize on the growing popularity within the Midwest scene, in early 1985, with the support of a group of local bike shops he conceived the MN (Minnesota) Freestyle Series.

The success of the MN Series contests became widely known. When Dale decided to expand on his idea after receiving strongly positive feedback, the new and ambitious Midwest Freestyle Series was born in the summer of 1987. The MFS, which immediately gained momentum, caught the attention of Bob Morales, owner of the high-profile American Freestyle Association. When an affiliation was formed between the MFS and the AFA, the relationship gave the MFS instant credibility. Moreover, Matson began to work locally on behalf of the AFA to increase local memberships and find suitable venues for more amateur contests. Within three years, AFA membership in the Midwest had grown from less than 100 to more than 400 actively competing riders.

The rapid growth in freestyle interest and participation throughout the 1980s was driven by the torrent of factory tours that plowed through the country each summer. Just in the summer of 1987, the established GT, Kuwahara, Diamond Back, General, Skyway, CW, and Haro teams left the surf and sun of California for America's heartland to capture the hearts, minds, and loyalty of their young target audience. It wasn't unusual for rival teams to appear at the same venue, on the same day, as shop owners seized the opportuniy to entice their locals with a full day of shows.

Alden Frostad pulls a "Funky Chicken" at the MFS Event in East St. Paul Armory in 1988.

Forest Lake local Gil Cornea competes at the 1988 at the MFS contest at the Church of Christ, Coon Rapids.

1988 - Ron Wilkerson - The master of the lip trick - Pulls a pedal picker drop in at Penn Cycle, Richfield, MN.

Brian Blyther with a clicks turndown/lookdown at Penn Cycle, Richfield, MN on the 1988 Haro Tour of Kings.

Street riding is often talked about as an evolution in freestyle that happened later in the decade, but it's actually how most of us started. We would search endlessly for new places to ride, and as our group grew in numbers the brigade became the focal point of the KC scene. Just about every local rider throughout the 1980s was at some point striving to join us. The list of those who rode on those long days and nights, and who helped to influence the scene in Kansas City, is far too extensive to recall in detail. Many riders who travelled through the region have great—and sometimes scary—memories of their time spent with our crew.

- Dennis McCoy

I sent out a hodgepodge of mailings to all the bike shops to bring in riders because I had decided to hold a series of local contests. The first happened in the summer of 1985 in Coon Rapids, Minnesota. Over 100 riders entered, and hundreds of spectators came out to that first event. It was a great success and spurred me on to organize another one the year after...

The first contests were all outdoors at participating bike shops around the state. In 1987 and in the years after, they were all held indoors at various venues around the Midwest, such as ice-skating arenas and National Guard armories. Rick Moliterno made several trips to MFS events and was always a crowd-pleaser. More than 40 individual contests were completed within those years.

The years 1986 to 1989 were the boom years of freestyle in Minnesota. Summer was our favorite time of year, as we would get to open at shows and ride with the Haro guys who were regularly touring and hanging out in the region. I remember one year when Dennis McCoy visited our local half-pipe while on a Haro tour and he busted an air so big, he was lost in the branches of an overhead tree!

The inspiration for us as kids in those early years was the magazines, which had pictures of tricks that everyone would try to duplicate. We brought those tricks into our back yards, and they would eventually make it to the outdoor shows that we arranged and held at local bike shops. The biggest impact of those years was seeing Bob Haro and his teams perform. Those Haro shows were magical, and along with Dyno, GT, and the rest of the teams of the era, they drove us on.

– Dale Matson

John Mulhouse pulls a backward bar slide at the 1987 Park Schwinn bike shop MFS event in White Bear Lake.

Such was the level of demand from bike shops when, that same summer, Haro Tour Manager Bill Hawkins decided to dispatch two touring teams within the US in a bid cover more ground. While the established team of Ron Wilkerson, Brian Blyther, and Dave Nourie began the summer on the West Coast, a new team consisting of Dennis McCoy, Rick Moliterno, and Joe Johnson set off for shows in the Midwest (where all three riders had grown up) and on the East Coast. Tour stops at bike shops in Minnesota, Wisconsin, and Indiana, as well as multiple shows in Ohio, Michigan, and Illinois, highlighted the importance of the Midwest region. With the debut AFA Masters Columbus Ohio contest at the end of the tour, the Midwest was officially a busy summer junction for the freestyle movement.

As the AFA began to fold down its tents in the late 1980s, an ambitious alternative contest series developed to take its place. Ron Wilkerson's 2Hip King of Vert series was created in

response to the belief that the AFA quarter-pipe-and-kick-turn ramp format was both outdated and unprogressive. The AFA, which had become a larger and less-flexible organization, was accused by a number of senior professional riders of losing touch with and even ignoring riders' opinions. In contrast to the regulated format of the Masters, the King of Vert series revolved around a more-relaxed jam format on a half-pipe ramp; as such it was welcomed by competitors as well as riders who were committed to making the events happen no matter what. With new devotion to the progress of vert riding, freedom of expression replaced point-scoring among riders who viewed themselves more as a brotherhood than a group of rivals. Thus the launch of the KOV series is fondly recalled as a genuine moment of reinvention for the sport. The first event of this series, which would continue and grow through the late 1980s and into early 1990, was held in a freezing pole barn in Lesueur, Minnesota. The rebirth of freestyle BMX had to happen somewhere, and clearly the Midwest was as good as any place on earth.

Bob Haro, America's number one freestyler gives the kids of Harrow something to talk about.

Bob Haro visits the UK's Harrow Skate Park in 1982 to promote the Haro Freestyler frame and fork.

BOB HARO

—LIVING LEGEND!

Report: **MARTIN HIGGINSON**
Picture: **DAVE FERGUSON**

When it comes to shakin' peoples hands, one bloke you ought to beware of is Bob Haro. Oh boy, talk about crushed fingers, that just 'aint in it! I thought it was a competition that they have in the States, so there I was trying to crush his hand too, but with little success. So folks if you find a few spelling mistakes lying in this interview, don't be alarmed, 'cos it's real difficult typing with four broken fingers.

Anyway, on with the interview which was no easy task, it's easier getting blood out of a stone than Bob Haro off those video games. Eventually after having him a few games, I coaxed him outside, the fact that Bob had run out of money helped the matter.

As ever, I blasted off with my usual intor' line!

BMXW: When did you first get interested in BMX?

B.H.: Well it was back in about '77, I started racing BMX along with my mates, on a square tailed Redline. As well as racing, I also started making number plates for my mates. Other kids at the race meetings liked them so I started to sell them. They cost around £7.50 which was reasonable for a good quality plate.

BMXW: What about the Haro Numbers, when did they start?

B.H.: Well it was round about the same time. The kids

> ### "I KNEW ALL THE TOP GUYS, SO I GAVE THEM A SPONSORSHIP, WHICH REALLY HELPED MY GEAR TO TAKE OFF"

started crying out for coloured numbers, so I started to cut fancy numbers out of contact. The kids loved them and just everyone had them.

BMXW: Did you make the plates and numbers to make money, in other words did you see this as a lucrative market?

B.H.: No, at first it was just to satisfy the needs of my mates, but at the end of '77, I went on tour with S.E. Racing and I only had about 50 dollars to last me so the only way to stay on the tour was to start making selling numbers and plates. I also started to produce some drawings, which I consequently sold to BMXA, you know the Stateside Mag. They really liked my stuff, and offered me a job doing artwork, drawing up adverts and the occasional bit of writing. It was real good fun.

BMXW: What about the stunt side of your life?

B.H.: Well this all started when I was working at BMXA, R. L. Osborn (Bob Osborn, the owner of BMXA's son) and myself always used to go practising together. We both loved freestyle and this was mainly what we concentrated on. After perfecting thousands of tricks we decided to start the BMXA stunt team, which performed demos' at many of the major races. The first show was in Arizona around '79.

BMXW: How come you left BMXA?

B.H.: Well we had a lot of problems, I wanted to spend more time on my own business and this just wasn't possible with BMXA. So after a long chat, Bob Osborn and myself agreed that it was time I made a break!

BMXW: What happened next?

B.H.: Well I'd made enough money to buy special tools in order to cut plates and numbers in large quantities. I then

Classy stuff, from the master himself, the one and only Bob H

had stickers made instead of making them myself.

BMXW: What about promoting your products?

B.H.: Well I knew all the top guys, so I gave them a sponsorship, which really helped my gear to take off.

BMXW: What about your drawing?

B.H.: Well BMX Plus offered me a part-time job doing the occasional drawing for them. I decided to take it. I now do a regular column for them all about freestyle, which helps both them and me! It's also great fun.

BMXW: Do you find that exporting your goods is worthwhile?

B.H.: Oh yes, in the U.K. they're just crazy for my gear, it's really good. The same is happening, but slower in

Europe, in fact the export market is really excellent moment, I just hope it stays that way.

BMXW: With all this business on your hands, do ye much time for practicing?

B.H.: Well, I try and practice around three days five, but it's real difficult, 'cos there's always ple work to be done.

BMXW: What happens when you go on tour?

B.H.: Well I've jsut employed a new bloke who deal

MORE ACTION OVERLEAF ..

7 | EUROPE

BMX first arrived in Europe during the late 1970s, brought home from the United States by European motorcycle racer Pierre Karsmaker and a group of journalists who had visited to compete in, and record, the action of California's frenetic motocross scene. In BMX they witnessed the green shoots of a new, unique concept that was quickly catching on among a group of young motocross fans. Not content to simply stand on the trails and watch as their idols passed in blurs of dust and two-stroke exhaust fumes, this group wanted to race––and they weren't alone. BMX quickly defined itself as an action sport for the young, competitive, and courageous, and by the turn of the decade it had found a captive audience within the United States.

Nicky Restall (pictured) and Tom Lynch both represented Haro in the UK race scene in 1987.

A period of development and promotion for BMX began to unfold across Europe in the spring of 1978. Having seen the opportunity in the US firsthand, Dutch motocross racer Gerrit Does started to network with the established BMX organizations on the East and West coasts with the goal of developing the best formula for the sport's introduction to Europe. His belief in and vision for the concept led to collaboration with a group of leading BMX brands and distributors; within a year, modest distribution channels for bikes, clothing, and equipment were in place. The Dutch Bicycle Motocross Federation, formed in 1978, staged its first regulated race in a schoolyard in Eindhoven in the spring of 1979. Not long after, Marcelle Seurat formed the French Federation of Bicrossing, which in early

1980 facilitated the country's first BMX race at a newly built track in Beaune. In the spring of 1980, bicycle and car accessories giant Halfords funded the design and build of the UK's first dedicated track. Located in Redditch near Birmingham, England's second-largest city, the track hosted the country's first official BMX race that August. The event was facilitated by the UKBMXA, a new organization set up by Halfords Cycling Brand Manager David Duffield. Italy soon followed suit when sports promoter and journalist Aldo Gandolfo founded the Italian BMX Association in December of 1981. A year later, the organization joined the larger International BMX Federation and staged its debut race in the historic Alpine town of Pinerolo.

As BMX began to connect with its audience in Europe, a flood of new magazines emerged. The UK's BMX Official became one of the first dedicated printed publications outside of the United States. After enduring a financially challenging debut year, the magazine abruptly disappeared in late 1981, but it reappeared in August of 1982 as the more evolved and appealing BMX Action Bike. Among Action Bike's freestyle riding features, which began immediately, a profile and interview with Bob Haro provided both a statement of intent and a sign of things to come. Exposure created demand: Bob Haro arrived in the UK in the summer of 1982 clutching his latest creation, the Haro Freestyler frame and fork. Across the Channel, in France, Moto Verte magazine

Jason Davies Elbow Glides on a Haro Master in the UK - 1988

underwent a similar evolution. The 1980 issue of this motocross magazine, featuring BMX, became a best seller and spawned Bicrossing (called Bicross by readers), a sister publication dedicated to the developing French BMX scene. Through the decade it would become a vital source of international BMX news in France as well as an advocate for the Haro brand.

The early 1980s were a pivotal era of development in the formative European freestyle scene. Bob Haro's return to the UK in the summer of 1983, to ride in a televised freestyle demonstration at Birmingham's National Exhibition Centre, had been eagerly awaited and inspired a more-evolved understanding of the freestyle concept. Through the middle of the decade, promotional visits from GT's Eddie Fiola and Bob Morales as well as the highly rated Haro freestyle team of Ron Wilkerson, Brian Blyther, and Dave Nourie continued to energize the scene in Europe. As the new sport became primed to explode, live exposure to US stars created a fanatical following for the leading freestyle brands.

The next logical step for the Europeans was the development and recognition of homegrown talent. Both the desire for legacy and a genuine future for freestyle were undeniable. As the European movement continued to build, exciting new opportunities began to emerge. In December of 1984, the passion and dedication of the growing French fan base was rewarded with the country's first international BMX race event, held in Paris at the giant indoor Palais Omnisport Bercy Arena. Facilitated and arranged by the AFB (French Association of Bicrossing) and sponsored by Bicross, the Bicross International event brought together the elite of the international scene for a weekend of intensely competitive racing. The main talking

In 1986 we rode alongside Mike Dominguez, Martin Aparijo, and the French Mad Dogs team of Adolphe Joly, and Jose and Michel Delgado at the bicross event at the Paris Bercy Omnisport Arena. We (Haro BLIX) also organized the first Masters of freestyle in Marseille, where the prizes were presented by two legends of Formula 1 racing: Didier Pironi and Jacques Laffitte. In 1987, I won the overall French Freestyle Champion Title. David Chabert became the Flatland Champion in the 16 and Under Expert category at the BMX Worlds in the UK in 1987 and Patrice (Kharoubi) and Christophe (Chevalier) had some success at the AFA Columbus, Ohio event in 1988. Christophe came fourth in vert, just behind Mat Hoffman, Carlo Griggs, and Joel Alamo. Between 1985 and 1989 we were highly active as a team, with tours of Africa, European contests, and summer tours through France with Brian Blyther, Ron Wilkerson, and Dave Nourie. It was a special time for us as kids growing up and we got to ride with a group of highly talented International riders.

– Jean Somsois

Bob Haro sent me a letter congratulating me after winning the Worlds in '88, saying he was so proud to have a rider like me representing the company. That blew me away.

– David Frame

David Frame won the BMX Freestyle Worlds event during his time as a Haro rider in the late 1980's Seen here on a 1991 Air Master in Scotland.

point, however, had little to do with what was happening on the track. GT's Eddie Fiola, King of the Skate Parks champion, along with BMX Action Trick Team rider RL Osborn, had been invited to the Bercy to give the crowd a close-up look at freestyle. The two Californians didn't disappoint, staging an impressive series of four individual demonstrations during intervals in the weekend schedule––and 13,000 young spectators were on hand to witness two of the world's finest freestyle riders in action. The success of this event would have a swift and decisive impact on the European freestyle scene. In the following weeks, widespread magazine coverage and national TV exposure brought the message to tens of thousands more

French teenagers. On a cold winter weekend in Paris, the dawn of a new era in French youth culture had begun at the Bercy Arena.

In October of 1985, the Haro Blix Freestyle Team was formed in the French town of Arles Préfecture. The original team consisted of six local riders: Patrick Roman (RIP 1970 - 2000), David Chabert, Patrice Kharoubi, Christophe Chevalier, Patrice Ginoyer, and Jean Somsois (the team captain). With the support of Haro's French distributor; V-2000 and the guidance and direction of team manager Philippe Roman, they embarked on a four-year period of freestyle promotion across France. The team played an important role in helping to establish freestyle at a local level in the country and would often team up with the US Haro team to carry out shows at bike shops and regional events.

The year 1984 became known as the "Year of Freestyle" in the UK. Haro's new star rider, Mike Dominguez, arrived in England with Bob Haro, and the two set out on a busy summer schedule of promotional appearances at skate parks and BMX shops around the country. A strained appearance on morning television saw Bob Haro defending the safety aspects of freestyle riding as interviewer Anne Diamond proclaimed that more than one million BMX bikes were in active use in England alone. A brief trip to Germany and Holland followed, during which the two stars performed freestyle demonstrations in shopping malls and bike shops, and at BMX races. Upon returning to the UK they headed to the Kellogg's BMX Race Championships in Newcastle, where Dominguez competed in a freestyle contest against his friend and rival Eddie Fiola and a group of rising British stars. Bob Haro participated, although without his bike, alongside his friend and former teammate Bob Morales on the judging panel.

Without a doubt, however, the most ambitious and decisive moment of 1984 for the UK scene took place that December. Entrepreneur and racer-turned-TV-presenter Andy Ruffel, who had figured prominently in the development of BMX in the UK by demonstrating enormous versatility as a successful BMX racer and capable freestyle rider, had recently created a vehicle for the national promotion of freestyle with a new venture he named Holeshot Promotions. His vision for ,and knowledge of ,the UK scene gave rise to an idea that would galvanize the UK freestyle movement at a moment in which it had momentum, but needed direction. Accordingly,

the UKBMX organization––with sponsorship and support from BMX Action Bike as well as Holeshot––facilitated the first recognized British Freestyle Championships, at the Michael Sobell Leisure Centre in North London. The event, a watershed moment for the UK scene, attracted a huge audience of young spectators and hosted just about every known or emerging rider in the nation.

The year 1985 included more growth opportunities for BMX freestyle in Europe. That December, TV coverage of the second Bicross International event, again held at the Bercy Omnisport Arena, introduced Haro pros Rich Sigur and Ron Wilkerson to the watching nation. The presence of the Haro Team in Europe created an interesting dynamic among the European riders, many of whom had spent the past two years studying pictures in BMX Action Bike of Mike Dominguez, Ron Wilkerson, Brian Blyther, and Dave Nourie. The Americans had motivated and inspired the emerging European riders; their exploits had been their introduction to freestyle. But the riders weren't the only ones looking west for inspiration. For freestyle to have a genuine future as a sport in Europe, it needed direction and leadership.

Also in December of 1985, a meeting took place in an ordinary office building in central London. The three individuals in attendance, all of whom had played central roles in steering and influencing the early UK BMX scene, were about to form the UK Bicycle Freestyle Association. Promoter and Skyway Team Manager Peter Hawkins, former head teacher and producer of the TV series BMX Beat Colin Kefford, and UKBMXA representative Sam Wood readily agreed to create an organization that would organize and regulate a series of freestyle

contests within the UK. But their immediate announcement of the logical introduction of a professional category, and the facilitation of a series of 17 individual regional and national freestyle contests to be held in 1986, became a point of contention within the national freestyle ranks. Disenchanted by the lack of rider involvement, a number of the senior riders saw the organization as arrogant and dictatorial–– concerns openly reported in the BMX press. Still, in spite of the doubters, the 1986 regional and national contest season would successfully drive the freestyle message to the four corners of the country. The season ended in December at the Michael Sobell Center in North London, where the Holeshot BMX Freestyle Championships saw Haro USA's rising star, Dennis McCoy, make a cameo appearance that lifted the roof off of the packed venue with his trademark quick feet and huge aerial variations. The UKBFA's busy first season had accomplished its objectives: a new breed of talent was emerging from the furthest corners of the country. The year ahead would be even more eventful.

With organized federations and associations now directing and facilitating freestyle contests across Europe, it was no surprise that the destination of the 1987 World BMX Masters was the UK. The "Worlds" concept had debuted the previous year in Vancouver, Canada, but typical teething problems and poor attendances, as well as a questionable scoring and judging system, had undermined the credibility of the event. But the sport's international governing body, the IBMXF, was not to be deterred. In the summer of 1987, the British were given a chance to host the Worlds, and in typical fashion they decided to make an impact. With the financial support of soft-drink company Tizer, the UKBFA decided to stage the event via a series of qualifying

Jason Davies, who rode on the UK Skyway Team, had been in my ear on a regular basis about why we didn't have a [Haro] team in the UK. Haro's presence as a brand in the UK market was obviously well established, and we had the backing of Haro USA who would help with product. The Skyway wheel was on its way out in the competitive scene and the Peregrine HP 48 wheel had become the lightest and strongest wheel on the market by late 1987. I couldn't imagine Skyway supporting a team that wasn't running the wheel, and with my guys gravitating towards the Haro brand, it seemed like an obvious next chapter for us.

– Peter Hawkins

Jason Davies became one of the first Haro UK Freestyle Team members in early 1988.

rounds to be hosted in six major UK cities over the course of six days. The teams and their riders were to be transported between locations on buses, and the televised finals would be staged on the seventh day in the English border town of Carlisle. Despite the lack of US rider involvement, and inevitable logistical problems, the event brought the best of the European freestyle scene to the fore. A rare European appearance from Skyway's prodigy Mat Hoffman helped the Skyway freestyle team to the title of World Factory Freestyle Champions in a series dominated by UK riders.

As the European scene evolved, so did the lifestyles of the riders. The impressionable kids who had been drawn to the sport in the early 1980s were now teenagers, with an appetite for independence and enough confidence to influence the direction of their lives. In the later decade, it wasn't unusual for sponsored riders to spend seven days a week riding, regardless of weather conditions and often in places far from home. Before long, a nationwide network began to trade intelligence on newly discovered riding spots or newly constructed back-yard ramps. On a daily basis, skate parks across Europe were under siege from hundreds of riders who routinely persevered through the best and worst of the European climate. However, regardless of the evolution of the scene, street riding remained the preferred method of experimentation. Infamous riding spots like London's South Bank, Cologne's spectacular cathedral concourse in Germany, and Paris's Trocadero brought together intensely committed groups from distant European locations, with the BMXers and skaters often coexisting in the spaces and feeding off of each others' energy.

In November of 1987, two rising stars of the UK Skyway Freestyle team embarked on a journey that would indirectly influence their destiny. Scott Carroll and Jason Davies had recently helped Skyway win the World Factory Freestyle Team title at the Tizer World Freestyle Championships in the UK; both had connections in the US through BMX. Using their summer earnings for airfare, they headed to California to ride and attend the AFA Masters contest series finals at the 7-Eleven Velodrome, south of Los Angeles. Having delivered the two riders to the airport, Team Manager Peter Hawkins decided that he too would like to travel and attend the event, and within 48 hours he was on a British Airways flight bound for LAX. The Masters finals were the event of the year in the US; both Bob Haro and Jim Ford were in attendance. A friendly discussion between Hawkins and the two Haro executives regarding the state of the UK freestyle scene took an inevitable turn when it focused on the conspicuous lack of a UK Haro team.

Back in the UK, Hawkins scheduled a meeting with Michael Allen at Shiner (Haro's UK distributor) to discuss the potential of the venture. Shiner, whose BMX sales were beginning to decline, was willing to promote Haro as a rival to the dominant UK Skyway Team in a bid to boost interest in freestyle. In early 1988, history was made when the first UK Haro Factory Freestyle Team was officially formed. Initially, four individual riders were selected as the basis of the team. Jason Davies, who needed very little persuasion to switch to his preferred brand, departed the Skyway team immediately. Scott Carroll, a Scotsman who had shown himself to be a hugely talented vert rider during the Tizer Worlds in 1987, also moved from Skyway to join Haro. Another promising young all-rounder named Karl Denton became the third

member, and super-smooth Scotsman David Frame jumped ship from the Mongoose brand to complete the lineup. Later in the year, following Carroll's departure, Texan vert rider Greg Guillotte joined the Haro team. Guillotte had moved to London via his father's international work placement and had announced his arrival on the UK scene in the summer of 1987 by winning the Master Class Vert category at the Tizer Worlds.

Haro's plans outside of the freestyle market were also beginning to look more ambitious. The brand had maintained a presence in the international BMX racing scene since the late 1970s with its widely used number plates, helmet visors, and race pants. In addition, the launch of the Haro Group 1 Race Bike in 1986 had created opportunities to develop a greater presence on the track. Next, in the spring of 1987 a co-sponsorship arrangement with seasoned British racers Nicky Restall and Tom Lynch was launched. Restall had raced on the early 1980s Diamond Back team in the UK–– a team managed and developed by Haro's UK Team Manager Peter Hawkins. When the opportunity to develop a UK race team for Haro arrived, Hawkins immediately identified Restall as a good fit. After a run of good results, Restall would become a fully sponsored Haro factory rider during the 1987 UKBMX race season.

Meanwhile, developments in the freestyle team were becoming more frenetic by the week. A successful UKBFA contest series throughout the summer of 1988 had put the new Haro team firmly on the map. Another UK-hosted World Freestyle Championship contest, held in Manchester, drew the sport's elite from mainland Europe, the UK, and the US. Reigning Under-15 World Ramp Champion David Frame once again dominated his age group by winning

Scott Carroll stood out as a gifted vert rider and joined Jason Davis as founder members of the UK Haro Team

Craig [Campbell] and I went over to California in 1988. We had been street riding a lot and Craig in particular wanted to get away from the squeaky-clean image of BMX that had developed in England. Spike Jonze and Andy Jenkins had heard we were coming out and wanted to do a piece in Freestylin' about the street-riding scene in the UK. We were both ex-skaters so were riding the South Bank a lot and making use of everything we could find. There was a great ledge at Highgate Train Station that we used to learn peg grinds and wall rides. When we got out to LA, we met with Spike and Andy and shot some sequences over at the famous Torrance and Santa Ana banks. That article appeared in Freestylin' in June of 1988.

– Jess Dyrenforth

We formed the BLIX (Bicycle Libre Expression) and became sponsored by the French Haro Importer V-2000. It started for us with the Bercy event in 1984; when Eddie Fiola and RL Osborne carried out an incredible freestyle demo on live TV.

— Jean Somsois

Taken by BLIX Team Manager Philippe Roman, Jean Somsois inverts at the 'Explorrateur Free" Show in Quimper, France in 1988.

the Worlds title, while Texan Greg Guillotte took first place in the Master Class Ramp category. Haro USA's Dennis McCoy and Joe Johnson dominated the professional ranks, with Johnson taking the title in the Pro Ramp division and McCoy taking the runner-up spot by a narrow margin. An additional, unconventional opportunity to promote the sport appeared in the form of a short-term contract at the Peter Jay Circus in Great Yarmouth. Greg Guillotte flew the flag for Haro for the three-month residency, during which Guillotte, Skyway's Mike Canning, and future Haro team rider James Hudson performed daily freestyle shows. Later, in November, Haro's David Frame, Skyway's Mike Canning, and brothers David and Brian Henderson all travelled to Monaco to perform a freestyle demonstration at the Monte Carlo International Circus Festival. The year quickly became even busier with circus events in Denmark, Italy, and West Germany, as well as a raft of personnel changes. After the hugely successful 1988 2Hip King of Vert Invitational Jam, held at the Bercy Arena in Paris, Scott Carroll departed the team. Another talented Scotsman, Steve Geall, was recruited to fill the void left by Carroll, but Texan Greg Guillotte was also on the move. When his father's work placement in Europe came to an end, the family packed up and headed back to the United States.

As the original team began to disband, a new group of talented riders lined up to represent Haro in the UK. The 1989 team welcomed brothers Mick and James Hudson as well as Ollie Matthews, Dave Blundell, Jason Ellis, and Sean Clark. The quality of the team and its continued improvement brought greater demand for promotional activities; a memorable one was the filming, in Amsterdam, of a TV commercial for Fristi (a yogurt drink). Residencies at the

Blackpool Circus in the UK and the Krone Circus in Germany became longstanding arrangements that led to Jason Davies and Mike Canning, along with new recruits Jason Ellis and Dave Blundell, relocating to Germany for six months of the year. An appearance on Paul Daniels' prime-time Magic TV Show incurred more mass exposure for the team when Sean Clark, James Hudson, and Dave Blundell rode in front of millions of viewers.

In 1989, a new sponsorship opportunity with Vision, a skateboard and streetwear company, became a watershed moment for the UK Haro team. As early as 1987, a group of core US riders had begun to discard the uniforms of their sponsors in what seemed like a streak of defiance, but in fact the move away from the corporate image simply demonstrated the growing divergence and lack of common vision between the industry and its athletes. When the late 1980s brought street riding back to the leading edge of the sport in what was now a well-connected global scene, a period of reinvention began. In the spring of 1988, Bicross brought Ron Wilkerson's innovative 2Hip King of Vert series to Paris. Based on a formula that disregarded almost every element of the early '80s AFA contest formats, the Half-Pipe Jam brought the world's best skaters and freestyle riders to the country's capital. The series seemed to crystalize the aspirations of the riders even as it showcased a new direction for the sport. The success of the 1988 event brought the 2Hip series back to Paris in February of 1989. Haro's Mat Hoffman and Brian Blyther both competed in the invitational that formed a part of the larger Mega Free 2 National Freestyle event.

But also during 1989, a far more worrying trend started to develop in the United States. Interest in BMX was in decline, reflecting the same plight

Haro UK's Texan import Greg Guillotte. Inverts, helmetless

The main things that were changing was that the BMX business was taking a dive in late '88 and by 1989, it was a serious situation. Skating was beginning to pick up again—skate had influenced BMX—and in the US, the BMX scene was heading into its street era. Freestyle definitely changed when the uniforms went and kids started wearing casual gear—Life's a Beach t-shirts and shorts—and as the guys were older now, there was a lot of interaction and traveling within the States, where the culture was evolving. It needed to happen and it was genuine evolution, but it started to lose its identity.

– Peter Hawkins

Haro UK's Ollie Matthews with a "Turn Down" down during a show at Yarmouth Circus in Eastern England.

that the global skateboard industry had experienced toward the end of the 1970s; accordingly, the domino effect began to set off alarm bells abroad. As the industry quickly retreated into what can only be described as survival mode, the relentless energy that had propelled the sport through the phenomenal growth of the 1980s was fading fast. But those who kept the faith would eventually be rewarded. Instead of quitting the sport due to the lack of sponsorship and salaries, riders appeared to feel not only unburdened but also empowered, and this new attitude re-energized the global scene. At the forefront of this new movement was Haro's US Pro Mat Hoffman, who began to push the boundaries of his ability beyond anything that the sport had ever witnessed or even dared to imagine. Within the six-month period between March and September of 1990, Hoffman pulled and landed two new tricks that helped to shape a new era in modern BMX. In March, his Flip Fakie in front of thousands of European fans at the 1990 Bicross International event at the Bercy was a game-changer. Then in September, at the UK King of Vert finals in Mansfield, England, he successfully landed the first-ever Flair in a contest––a trick he had quietly conceived and developed on his own ramp in Oklahoma.

Despite continuous innovation at the hands of the riders, however, by the end of the decade the backward trend was past the point of no return. The industry was in a state of flux, which put diversification and reinvention high on the agendas of the global brands that had identified the booming mountain-bike category as a safe haven. After a successful 1989 Worlds event in St. Ouen, France, where British riders won six of the eight overall categories, reinvention was also on the agenda at the UKBFA. Soon, deep disagreements about the future direction of the UK scene began to surface among the board members. Certain people within the organization felt that change was risky while others, including Hawkins, felt that it was essential.

Having taken a step away from the formulaic organization of the UKBFA, the UK scene began to work in smaller, independent groups to stage contests like the King of Concrete, a series that ran throughout the 1990s and attracted the best riders of the international scene. The World Freestyle Masters events were also now in the hands of riders, who were able to influence the culture of the sport throughout the 1990s and create an environment for innovation and evolution at events staged across Europe. New riders were continually emerging, and magazines including the UK's Invert (which would eventually become Ride UK), France's Bicross and Skate, and relative newcomer Freedom BMX (founded in Germany in 1993) continued to energize the subcultural scene and prove that without lucrative sponsorship deals or prize money, freestyle in Europe was alive and well.

The US scene was a direct influence on the scene in Europe. Ron Wilkerson was staging street and half-pipe contests, and our contests were still in quarter-pipe and flatland format. Away from the contests, the best riders were riding half-pipes and that is where we needed to go. We couldn't agree and I disconnected from the UKBFA soon after.

– Peter Hawkins

Scott Carroll with a classic look-back. Shot by Mark Noble for Invert Magazine, somewhere near Southampton in the UK.

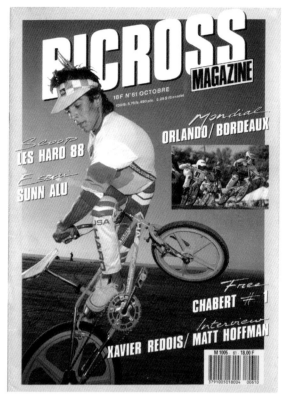

Haro's French connection - David Chabert (Top) and Jean Somsois, regularly featured in French BMX Magazine "Bicross."

Haro's Mat Hoffman pulls off the seemingly inconceivable. The first "Flair" ever to be successfully landed in a contest at the UK king of Vert In Mansfield, UK.

When Mat [Hoffman] came over to the UK in 1987, it was a useful moment for us. The UK Skyway Team was one of the best in the country. We were all aware of Mat's quality and it felt like a good idea to bring him into the mix here for the Tizer Worlds in 1987 to add some extra fizz. Initially, he wasn't very comfortable; no doubt [the visit was] a big culture shock for a young lad from rural Oklahoma. He did settle after a few days though and we saw the best of him and it was well worth it. I actually missed getting him to the airport on time for his flight home, which was a tense moment, but he was on his way a few hours later.

– Peter Hawkins

8 | SKATE

With Eben Krackau and Jim Gray

During the early summer of 1986, Bob Haro and Jim Ford hatched a plan that, if successful, was poised to redefine the future of the Haro brand in the action sports industry. Since the emergence of BMX freestyle, Haro had delivered a series of products and innovations that had quickly positioned the brand at the leading edge of the new sport. Therefore, it was entirely conceivable that the scheme developed around the boardroom table in Carlsbad would enable the company to apply its strengths and vision to the compact, lucrative skateboard scene.

Based on the creative skills and entrepreneurial mindset of Bob Haro, as well as the knowledge and industry experience brought by early skateboard innovator Jim Ford, Haro Designs soon embarked on 18 months of activity and promotion that would end in frustration.

However, the attempt did win over some of the skate community: the formation of Haro's Pad team, which featured some of the most iconic skaters in the history of the sport: Lance Mountain, Lester Kasai, Allen Losi, Billy Ruff, Mike McGill, and Christian Hosoi. Before long, ex-G&S pro Jim Gray would become the first and only professional skater to represent the Haro brand in its 36-year history.

The Haro Circuit Board was one of several that bob Haro designed and released in 1986

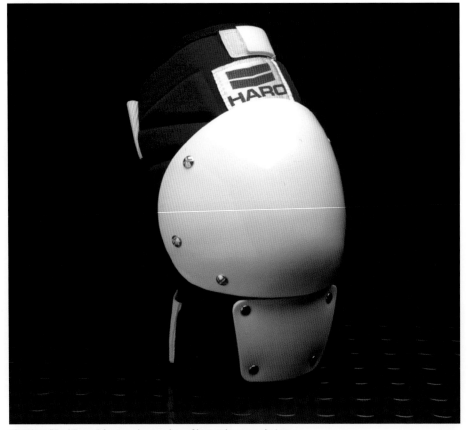

The Haro "Pad Team" featured a number of legendary pro skaters.

EK: How did your connection with Haro begin?

JG: I believe it was 1986 or 1987 when I quit G&S. I had no literal plan at the time, but I was concerned about how out of touch G&S was becoming with its skateboarding roots. It felt to me as if they were putting all of their resources into becoming a surf-clothing brand, so I went looking for something new. I was riding on the Haro Pads team and regularly popping into the office in Carlsbad to chat with Bob Haro and his marketing guy Jim Ford. Bob and I really clicked and developed a mutual respect pretty quickly. During one of those visits, and possibly helped by the fact that now they had access to a pro rider, they decided they wanted to make skateboards and they asked me if I'd ride for the brand. I can't recall remember too many of the details of how it went down, but I liked them and they liked me. So it began.

EK: How did Haro convince you to join up and how did you feel about the brand?

JG: We had a relationship through the pad deal so the timing worked well. I was a free agent, having left G&S, and it just flowed naturally into the board deal. I liked the brand; it seemed like they really cared about style. Bob was a great designer. And they had a great reputation in the BMX world. They treated us pretty well on the pad side of things, and I felt very at home with Jim and Bob. In fact, I was probably more comfortable with their personalities and their professional approach to working with me than most of the other brands I had been around in the skateboard business.

EK: What was it like coming from an established skate brand like G&S to skate for a BMX freestyle brand?

JG: The only real difference from a skating perspective was probably the portable quarter-pipes in the parking lot for BMX demos. I rode demos on Gale Webb's ramps from the age of 14, so I was already used to riding with guys like Eddie Fiola and this wasn't all that different. I had many other friends and respected skaters riding on the Haro Pad team with me––guys like Allen Losi, Lester Kasai, and Lance Mountain. In fact, Haro had much nicer facilities...cleaner and more organized offices than the skate companies, and that appealed to me. They treated us fine, but since the board program came and went so fast I can't really talk about how it played out compared to other brands I had been sponsored by.

EK: How did your peers and industry people feel about you skating for a BMX brand? In a time when skateboarders and BMX riders didn't exactly get along, did it feel like a gamble to sign with the leading BMX freestyle brand?

JG: I don't remember much heckling or any smack talk. It was in fact a bigger and more organized company than many of the skate brands at the time, so it was hard to be negative about it. I am sure there were doubters, and under-the-breath remarks, like the people who talked shit about Tracker trucks vs. Indy trucks. When people like that open their mouths and say negative things, they usually can't back it up, so I never really worried too much. I guess I was used to going against the grain; I respected people and companies for what they brought to the sport. So in a way I was the perfect guy to ride for them, because I already didn't march to the same drum as many skaters who were more concerned about image and who they were seen with than anything else. That was never my deal. I liked the guys at Haro and they liked me.

Jim Gray became the only skater to have a signature pro model deck designed by Bob Haro.

I have the original sketch of my graphics for my Haro board. I also have several of the boards in my collection in various different colors, and somewhere I have brand-new pads in the packaging. Mostly I have good memories of a fun time of life!

– Jim Gray

Although Haro appeared to have the support of a number of high profile skaters, the trade had other ideas.

We liked doing what we were doing and that was all I needed to get involved.

EK: I know there were a ton of rumors around mid-1986 linking Haro to other big-name pros. To your knowledge, was there a plan to have a full-on Haro skate team?

JG: I'm not sure, but it would have made sense. Having only one pro and one pro-model board was pretty minimal. Haro was a major player that I expected would have gotten in a lot deeper if Bob and Jim had continued to have full control of the direction and finances. It was during my involvement that the company was bought up by West Coast Cycle, and they had different ideas.

EK: I heard a rumor that G&S actually helped Haro to get their boards manufactured and screened. Is there any truth to that? At the time I remember seeing a lot of the G&S team skating in Haro pads.

JG: The biggest point of clarification is that G&S didn't actually manufacture skateboards; Watson Laminates or Taylor Dykema, in San Diego, made them. There were also a couple of contract screen shops that printed boards back then, so probably they were made side by side in the same factories. That would have confused people into thinking that G&S actually had something to do with board production. To my knowledge they did not.

EK: You had the only pro model board that Haro produced. Did you design your shape and influence the graphics? Your Haro board definitely resembled the boards that started to come through in the late 1980s.

JG: I definitely approved the shape. I don't think I actually drew it out on a template, but it was

my shape made to my requested specs. Bob showed me some ideas he had in mind for graphics and I liked them. They were unique on their own, and certainly different from what was already out there. I liked that approach. The whole line was very clean and reeked of Bob Haro styling, which for the most part was fine with me.

EK: Were you the only person to truly skate for Haro, other than the guys on the Pad team? Were there any amateur skaters with the brand?

JG: I was the only one who rode a Haro board. I think the skate program was so short-lived that they never really got that side of it together. They were in the process of selling the company at the time. The skaters weren't aware of that, but it must be hard to develop something so major with so much going on behind the scenes.

EK: Do you have any keepsakes from your time with Haro?

JG: I have the original sketch of my graphics for my Haro board. I also have several of the boards in my collection in various different colors, and somewhere I have brand-new pads in the packaging. Mostly I have good memories of a fun time of life!

EK: What was your overall opinion of the skate pads?

JG: I'd give them a 15 on a scale of 10 for design and appearance because they were approached so differently than all the pads that had been made up to that point. They looked great and they were light, which was appealing to me as a skater. As for safety and impact...they got more of a 6 out of 10. Didn't quite do the job we had hoped for!

Lester Kasai features in the Haro knee and elbow Pad advert.

EK: Did you ever spend time with the BMX team?

I would run into Ron Wilkerson here and there, but other than that we didn't cross paths too often. It was a strange time in skateboarding. I didn't actually go to a lot of demos and contests while I rode for Haro.

EK: Considering the untimely demise of Haro Skateboards, how do you look back on your time with the company?

JG: I have nothing but good memories, and my experience with the company played into everything that happened next in my life in the world of skateboarding. When I see Bob Haro today, it's all smiles and good memories. Seeing old pictures of me with the pads on also makes me happy. They were good times with good people. I feel really fortunate to have been included in part of Bob and the Haro brand's history.

Haro's first, and only professional skater Jim Gray, carves a "Front side channel air", at the Vancouver Worlds Fair contest in 1986.

This was a market that neither Jim nor Bob fully understood at the time, and the Explorer was born ou of the simple tactic to go to market with 'something.'

– Dean Bradley

1987. Bob Haro and Marketing Manager Trish Walsh shoot for the Haro "All Terrain" catalogue..

Dean Bradley pictured on the cover of Haro's first dedicated "All terrain" Catalogue.

SHIFT INTO HARO

Haro EXPLORER all-terrain cycles. 20 inch, 24 inch, and 26 inch multispeed bikes built to take you anywhere. Because sooner or later, you'll make the shift.

Haro Cycles, Inc.
6066 Corte Del Cedro
Carlsbad, CA 92008
(619) 438-4812

explorer

Haro's first for offering into the All Terrain market was a "White label" frame and fork named the "Explorer."

9 | MTB

ALL TERRAIN ASSAULT

The true origins of off-road cycling can be traced back to the evolution of cyclocross racing. During the 1940s, when extreme winter weather conditions in Europe forced road cyclists to consider alternative ways to stay fit outside of the traditional, competitive road-cycling season, riders began to adapt their road machines for the uneven tracks and pathways that led away from the frozen tarmac. Cyclocross quickly became a recognized category of competitive cycling, and in the early 1950s a world championship race series began that would increase popularity and create a worldwide following for the new sport.

The Klunkers

During the 1970s, groups of cycling enthusiasts in regions of northern California began to experiment with an idea that was radically different from the existing road-cycling scene. First they made basic modifications to the widely available, heavy balloon-tire-cruiser-style bicycles by adding more-suitable tires and multiple gear ratios to produce early hybrids that were fondly known as "klunkers." As the modifications became more ambitious, the creators of these concept bikes began to stage organized events and competitive races that gradually drew a whole new group of people into the experimental off-road scene. By the late 1970s, individual groups––in different, but

equally challenging and treacherous regions of the world––were busily developing similar ideas. This parallel period of development in off-road cycling would converge in a single outcome: the arrival of the mountain bike.

The very first complete mountain-bike model was developed and manufactured in 1977; this was a prototype called Breezer 1, produced in the US by rider, enthusiast, and designer Joe Breeze. In the late 1970s, a number of the European brands began to produce frames that utilized standard road-bike geometry, with modified interfaces to accommodate larger tires and sturdier components. In the summer of 1981, a US brand called Specialized launched the first mass-produced complete mountain bike, the Stumpjumper. The bike, which retailed for $750 in 1981, utilized the relatively new manufacturing technique known as TIG welding and carried a range of custom, Specialized-brand mountain-bike parts. The frame and fork featured dedicated all-terrain geometry, a logical step that would define the new category and set it even farther apart from the road and cyclocross disciplines. The release of the Stumpjumper played a key role in legitimizing the sport of mountain biking for a wider audience and also made a statement for Specialized that would drive a feverish period of research and development among the larger established

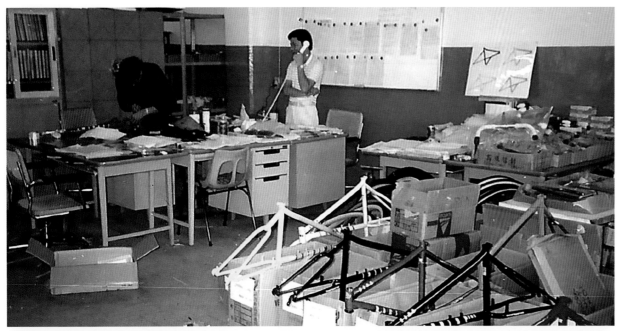

Bob Haro at the Southern Cross factory in Taiwan, dressing the" All Terrain" frames with his latest artwork.

Bob Haro and legendary Action Sports photographer James Cassimus shooting for the Haro "All Terrain" catalogue.

bicycle brands. Once, mountain-bike riding had been considered nothing more than a passing craze by those in the corporate offices of the wider bicycle industry. But by the early 1980s, the mountain bike had arrived in spectacular fashion, and the direction of the established bicycle industry was about to change as a result.

In response to the escalating interest in mountain-bike riding, Haro Designs began to consider an off-road model as early as 1984. Haro General Manager Jim Ford, a native Coloradan, kept a close eye on the developing scene and, in a moment of clarity, took his idea to company founder and president Bob Haro. Haro's first tentative step into the mountain-bike market came in 1985, during a period of substantial growth in the relatively new 20-inch BMX freestyle category. Despite the exciting prospect offered by this new direction, however, the company lacked the resources to pursue the developing market with anything other than a token gesture.

The 1986 Haro Explorer line was developed in partnership with Anlen, Haro's Taiwanese BMX manufacturer and assembler. Essentially, the Explorer was an off-the-shelf, white-label chromoly frame and fork, assembled with a mixture of Asian components that were sourced via the Taiwanese Bicycle Guide. Available in three sizes––20-, 24-, and 26-inch––the Explorer comprised the full extent of the Haro mountain-bike line until Bob Haro brought new expertise to the company in January of 1987.

In late 1986, Dean Bradley left his role as editor of BMX Plus! magazine. An avid action sports enthusiast and mountain-bike racer, Bradley had recently published the debut issue of Mountain Bike Action magazine for the Hi-Torque Publications media group. His knowledge of the mountain-bike scene, and his connections within

NORBA Trials champion Kevin Norton was a friend of Haro's MTB Brand Manager Dean Bradley. Norton helped develop the Haro "Response" Trials model in 1987.

it, would bring an immediate level of expertise to Haro and lead to a more specialized and ambitious future for its mountain-bike range.

With these new developments, 1988 became Haro's breakthrough year. In addition to the specialist and entry-level models that Bradley had slated and went on to develop in his first few months at the company, Haro further broadened its model range with the introduction of two mid-level mountain bikes: the Instinct and the Impulse. Another brand-new concept was a bicycle-trials bike, the Haro Response. The Response was developed with the help and input of Kevin Norton, the 1985/86 NORBA (National Off-Road Bicycle Association) U.S. Trials champion. Norton, a friend and neighbor of Bradley, was also a former motorcycle-trials rider who became the first recognized star of the U.S. Bicycle Trials riding scene in its conceptual year. At the 1988 Inter-Bike Trade Show in Long Beach, California, Haro distributed a dedicated four-page brochure and presented its newly improved and expanded mountain bike line to the trade. Other developments and refinements in 1989 included an expanded eight-page brochure and a series of dedicated magazine advertisements that emphasized the company's commitment to the category.

During this period, several members of the BMX Racing Team, including decorated and senior professional riders Mike King and Pete Loncarevich and NBL/ABA Girls Junior Cruiser champion Tara Llanes, all expressed interest in racing in the 26-inch wheel category; as a result, a formative Haro mountain-bike racing team was loosely formed. Because the transition between the two competitive disciplines was relatively easy, through the late 1980s a considerable number of BMX racers would make the obvious step into MTB and, in most cases, have an immediate impact in competition.

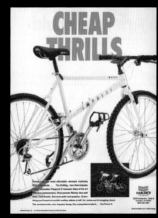

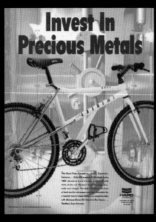

A selection of Haro adverts from the late 1980's and early 1990's.

When I joined Haro in early 1987, I was tasked with developing a more complete, less off-the-shelf mountain-bike line, which we subsequently debuted a year later at the Long Beach Inter-Bike Show in January of 1988. The new line was still produced at Anlen, with the exception of the new Escape 20-inch and 26-inch models—the Escape was basically an unchanged, renamed Explorer. All frame geometries and designs were updated and made our own by incorporating a variety of modern features including rear monostays, wrap-around head gussets, and chainstay-mounted u-brakes. For the flagship model, the new Extreme, Bob Haro designed a radical new Triagonal, a triple-triangle frame design that incorporated a dramatically sloping top tube along with a very short head tube and fork steerer.

All of the frames were still produced from 100% chromoly steel, but Bob had designed—at the same time as rival brand Yeti—a radical, elevated-chainstay frame. Combined with some groundbreaking paint and graphics, the new models really cemented Haro as an innovative and progressive mountain bike brand.

– Dean Bradley

The following year, 1990, became a pivotal year for the company's ambitions within the all-terrain cycling scene. Energized by positive feedback, Haro responded confidently to the needs of the market, which launched a period of innovation both in bike design and new technology. The 1990 Haro Mountain Bike Catalogue evinced the company's serious intent by featuring a more-advanced range of bikes that would continue to build interest and confidence in a market that was not only growing rapidly but also becoming more complex by the year. The increased level of interest began to pose new challenges, however. The welcome uptick in demand for Haro's adult ranges placed a serious strain on the relationship between Haro and Anlen, its longstanding Taiwanese manufacturing partner. Anlen had become a recognized specialist in the manufacture and assembly of BMX bikes, but limitations in tooling, technology, and capacity were starting to cancel out Haro's efforts to capitalize on the growing opportunity offered by the adult category. By the end of the year, a different Taiwanese factory, Kenstone Metals, would become the exclusive manufacturer of the Haro adult ranges. In addition, the ranges would be overhauled and reinvented once again, to demonstrate the company's ambition and innovative vision for the all-terrain category.

Perhaps the most challenging development in the mountain-bike market at the beginning of the 1990s centered upon the evolution of, and the measurable gains contributed by, the use of alternative of raw materials. Almost every brand within the established market was preoccupied with weight and performance, and a period of intense research and development was underway in search of the next advantage. Aluminum frames were still the domain of a few specialist custom, US-based boutique brands like Ventana, Cannondale, and Klein, but the

industrious and highly motivated Taiwanese were determined to overcome the dynamic challenges and were beginning to produce positive results. But during 1992, outside forces began to take their toll and the future of the brand was threatened when Haro's parent company, Derby Cycle International, faced severe financial difficulties brought on by the protracted and unsuccessful relaunch of its Raleigh worldwide brand. Still, with typical confidence, Haro overcame these challenges in by early 1992 had introduced the all-aluminum-framed Extreme AL as well as a new hybrid 7000, alloy front-triangle/ 4130 bolt-on rear-triangle mountain-bike named the Extreme Comp. Also offered was an elevated chainstay-titanium frame that was produced on behalf of Haro by US-based aluminum specialists Litespeed. Throughout the early 1990s, Haro continued to pursue the very best manufacturing options available and developed productive partnerships in Taiwan with Fung Tien, A-Pro, and Tai Huei and in the US with Kinesis, Litespeed, and Kastan Engineering.

For Haro's first foray into the full-suspension mountain-bike market, the company sought the guidance of Bryson Martin at specialty-fork manufacturer Marzocchi, in Bologna, Italy, which was already collaborating with its neighbor: legendary motorcycle frame-builder Verlicchi. The latter company had a formidable reputation within the motorcycle industry, having produced frames for legendary Italian brands including Ducati and Bimota; thus it was more than capable of producing what Haro visualized. Dean Bradley quickly began to focus on the next milestone for the Haro all-terrain range, and soon an ambitious new concept that he called the Haro Extreme FS (full suspension) was on the drawing board. The challenge of working with the Italians, which largely revolved around the

1993 - Team Haro MTB rider Michael Bohannon prepares to time trial at a NORBA event in Mammoth, CA.

Mountain bike conceptual's at the Southern Cross factory.

low volume of products required by Haro, meant deciding how the two companies could work together while maintaining an operating profit margin. Discussions with rival US mountain-bike brands, including Diamond Back and later, Iron Horse, were conducted in a bid to consolidate the partners' needs. Although communication with the Italians ultimately proved difficult and manufacturing challenges with Verlicchi ultimately resulted in the abandonment of the project, the Haro Extreme FS model was featured on the opening page of the 1993 Haro All-Terrain Catalogue.

As interest in off-road cycling continued to thrive throughout the 1990s, the Haro mountain bike ranges went from strength to strength, not only keeping pace with the quickly evolving market but also finding new and unique ways to capitalize on its established position. Mountain-bike racing had become a internationally recognized, mainstream sport, so a raft of new brands emerged and began to stake their own claim to innovative, forward-thinking designs and technologies, in a bid to win new business.

The off-road craze that had begun in the late 1970s was here to stay, and through visionary leadership and new expertise, Haro Designs had evolved to become a genuine bike brand. Although the company would continue to focus and innovate in the recovering BMX market in the years ahead, its forays into the MTB category had been a revelation––a new direction that may well have averted a disaster for the company.

Tara Llanes transitioned from Champion BMX racer, to off road contender with relative ease.

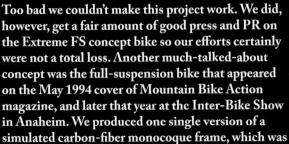

Bob Haro, top right of shot, observes frame builders at the Anlen factory in 1987.

Too bad we couldn't make this project work. We did, however, get a fair amount of good press and PR on the Extreme FS concept bike so our efforts certainly were not a total loss. Another much-talked-about concept was the full-suspension bike that appeared on the May 1994 cover of Mountain Bike Action magazine, and later that year at the Inter-Bike Show in Anaheim. We produced one single version of a simulated carbon-fiber monocoque frame, which was co-designed by myself and a local San Diego-area composite guy named David Beard. The bike was purely conceptual, but became a great press bike. It was designed and conceptualized with the intention of drawing attention to Haro's wide-open thinking when it came to full suspension on mountain bikes.

– Dean Bradley

Joe Johnson stretches a "Looks back" at the 2Hip King of Vert Finals, 1987, Leucadia, CA.

10 | JOE JOHNSON

As Joe Johnson rose through the ranks of the New England freestyle scene during the early 1980s, he joined a group of BMX racers in the region who would transition into freestyle with relative ease. Born and raised in the town of Stoughton, a suburb of Boston, Joe's lifestyle revolved around racing at his local track with a like-minded crew who had become captivated by the BMX phenomenon. After honing their racing skills, these young riders would soon become preoccupied with dirt jumping. Growing coverage of the developing West Coast freestyle scene in the BMX press offered an alternative direction and a wealth of new possibilities. Many of the committed faithful would become totally absorbed and never return to the track.

I started off racing BMX locally in around 1980. I became more interested in just dirt jumping and built a series of jumps in the woods behind my mom's house. I remember when freestyle began to appear in the magazines and a few kids began to experiment in parking lots and at race meets doing rock walks and rollbacks. I built my first quarter-pipe against two pine trees before I saw one in person. The suspense of what it would be like to ride that thing as we build it was unbearable. It started at 8 inches tall and eventually went to 9 inches tall after I was able to reach the top and started hanging up. We had a blast riding it, but it was obvious when we finished that we ignored any quarter-pipe building how-tos that we may have seen.

– Joe Johnson

In the summer of 1982, a rumor began to circulate in and around Boston about the existence of a wooden ramp somewhere in the area. Upon learning of its exact location, Johnson and his friends journeyed to a neighborhood across town to see it for themselves—and, hopefully, get permission to ride it. The construction they found was basic: a wooden deck resting against an above-ground swimming pool. Their journey had served a purpose, however. Within 24 hours, Joe and his friends had begun to construct their own ramp in the woods behind his mother's house. A beam about 8 feet off the ground was secured between two conveniently positioned trees, after which a ramp only slightly less sketchy was assembled from wood scraps that had been salvaged from friends' yards and garages. Over the next 18 months, the ramp evolved with the availability of better timber and eventually became an ideal venue for early freestyle experimentation. Then, in late 1984, the opportunity to completely re-engineer the ramp came via some useful advice from an expert source. Local promoter Ron Stebenne had invited GT's Eddie Fiola and Bob Morales to judge an amateur freestyle contest at a community center in Whitinsville, Massachusetts. When Johnson approached Fiola for advice on ramp construction, Fiola directed him to a set of plans that had been published in BMX Action and explained the "string and pencil" method of creating the perfect transition.

Johnson inverts one footed with typical effortless style.

We built an 8-foot quarter-pipe with a roll-in that went 'way back into the woods on sheets of plywood. The ramp eventually developed into a half-pipe, and went 'way back into the woods on sheets of plywood. The ramp eventually developed into a half-pipe, and our lifestyle consisted of six to eight guys who were all passionate about freestyle, riding, and sessioning in any spare time we had. That was the period where I really progressed as a rider. On weekends we would actually get fairly big crowds coming to the house. I thank my mom for letting me turn the back yard into a sea of plywood.

- Joe Johnson

Johnson clicks a stylish lookback. Luecadia, 1987. King of Vert finals.

suggested that Johnson supply some video footage for Bill and Bob Haro to assess. This suggestion posed an immediate problem (Joe didn't have or even know anybody who had a video camera) but his friends and fellow riders recognized the magnitude of the opportunity. After an appeal for help was made to numerous sources, a camera was located and a short riding edit submitted.

December of 1985 brought with it the opportunity that Joe Johnson had been hoping for. A month before the AFA Masters finals in Manchester, New Hampshire, Bob Haro confirmed that his company would enter into a 12-month co-sponsorship arrangement and gave Joe the go-ahead to begin representing the brand in competition. When news of an impressive debut at the Master's––second place in the Expert Ramp Class–– made its way back to Haro headquarters in Carlsbad, Bob Haro upped the ante in recognition of Joe's obvious talent. The new arrangement paid a monthly salary but required Johnson to tour. It wasn't a difficult decision, but did require some negotiation.

In April of '86, Haro called and asked me to fly to Florida because Tony Murray had sprained his knee at a show and was heading back to California. I was flown down to join up with Rich Sigur and Dave Nourie. We started in Florida, with a schedule that took us onto Georgia and then to Bermuda. I was in high school and I asked my teachers if I could do my finals early and they agreed. I said, 'So long, suckers!' to my friends. I couldn't believe it was happening. I flew to Florida and during the first show Rich asked me to do a Double Air. It went badly wrong and I carved off the side of the ramp, landed on my front wheel and broke my wrist! By Monday I was back in high school with a cast on my arm. My friends had plenty to say. It was heart-wrenching!

– Joe Johnson

As his riding ability improved, Johnson began to participate in the increasing number of local freestyle contests. With the expansion of Bob Morales's AFA contest organization out of the established West Coast scene, plus a series of collaborative local amateur freestyle contests aimed at developing new and emerging talent, there were more and more opportunities to ride and get noticed. Johnson competed in a half-dozen AFA contests held in local National Guard armories through the 1985 contest season and quickly became recognized as a rider with natural ability. But his real breakthrough came by way of a high-profile visitor. Haro's Ron Wilkerson had traveled to New England to stay with his East Coast teammate Paul Delaiarro ahead of an AFA contest in Fitchburg, Massachusetts. Paul suggested that Ron might like to meet his friend Joe, whom he had gotten to know through the local contest scene, and ride the infamous Johnson backyard half-pipe.

I think he [Ron] was just being a good guy by showing up and riding with us but I was so psyched to meet him. We were all set at the house waiting for them to arrive. They pulled in and it was like, 'Oh my God, he's here— act normal, act normal.' But I really felt like I was on my game that day, and Ron offered to help me out with a recommendation to Bob Haro.

– Joe Johnson

After the session, Wilkerson was impressed enough to hand Johnson a Haro jersey, which Johnson would wear in the Fitchburg contest a few days later. With the promise of a recommendation to Bob Haro on his return to California, Wilkerson departed, and within a few weeks Haro's Bill Hawkins was on the phone with a request. Bill needed some visual evidence of Johnson's ability to justify a commitment from Haro, so it was

Well known for his style, it's Joe Johnson's stubbornness that brought us the Tail-Whip Air. I watched him try it countless times in Europe in the summer of '88, and it didn't look like it was going to happen. It did, though—at the very next AFA comp. Amazingly, he would pull the first Double Whip only seven months later.

– Dennis McCoy

Another major breakthrough: Johnson became the first rider to land the tail whip air, redirecting the future of the sport in a single moment.

I used to watch Joe riding, and he owned this whole different category of style and flow. I never really looked at it from a judging perspective; I just knew I would never ride like that. I rode my way and he rode his way, and when we competed it was always really tight. I could never call it before the judges announced the winner of some of those battles; in fact, I mostly thought that Joe probably should have won. He just had this awesome natural flow and rhythm and was great to watch from the deck.

– Mat Hoffman

The broken wrist kept Johnson off his bike for a prolonged period, but having gotten so close to his dream of touring with the legendary Haro team, his determination to come back was never in doubt. The timely expansion of Ron Wilkerson's 2Hip King of Vert contests in 1987 offered plenty of opportunities to ride and compete, but now another significant challenge lay ahead. Johnson's Expert Ramp Division included another young up-and-coming rider with serious ability named Mat Hoffman. The two were similar in that they were both gifted and highly respected, although their riding styles were almost completely opposite. The two would go head-to-head in the 2Hip King of Vert throughout the 1987 contest series.

In June of 1987, Johnson was given a second chance at life on the road as a member of the Haro Freestyle Team. Haro's Rampage Tour would take two separate teams on a three-month journey around a vast region of the United States. Johnson was teamed up with Dennis McCoy and Rick Moliterno, two riders he knew well and with whom had spent time riding away from the contest scene. Also on board was Australian announcer Nick Jonze, who would ultimately leave the tour by popular demand and be replaced by the more-experienced Jon Peterson.

Back in California, the new 2Hip King of Vert contest series was expanding with the riders' vision for the sport's future. A steep upward curve in ability and progress was breaking new ground in the sport. Accordingly, as he continued to improve and transition to the half-pipe format, Johnson prepared to step up to the professional division. His future as a Haro rider was also under consideration. Since his ill-fated first Haro tour, Johnson had become friendly with Haro teammate Dennis McCoy, who was in the form of his life and well on the way to the numerous titles and awards he would claim for his performances in the 1987 season. McCoy, however, decided that he needed to capitalize on his form and working with Micki Conte, a sports agent who had recently secured a lucrative contract for Eddie Fiola with Levi Strauss & Co. the world-famous jeans manufacturers. The two began looking at the opportunities outside of the flagging BMX market, and in late 1987, McCoy introduced Johnson to Conte with a view to a similar arrangement.

scenario, For her part, Conte began to reach out and regularly reported back to her two clients. In an ambitious scenario, she would negotiate with and manage a group of sponsors: sportswear giant Adidas, which would provide footwear and clothing, and car a dealership that would supply each rider with a vehicle. The most significant deal, however, would involve the mass-market bicycle brand Huffy. Eager to gain entry to and credibility within the popular freestyle market, Huffy agreed to a lucrative sponsorship that would bring both McCoy and Johnson to the brand as pro riders. In the absence of a performance freestyle bike in their line, Mexico-based bike manufacturer Kastan would produce custom chromoly frames for the two riders that would allow them to compete at the highest levels without the hindrance of outdated geometry.

After dragging on for months, the two riders' negotiations with Haro had become static. So, after an offer from Haro accompanied by an ultimatum, McCoy and Johnson opted to put faith in their agent and in early 1988 officially signed with Huffy in a Kansas City escrow office. Unfortunately, the lack of a third-party signature from their agent kept the deal from being legally binding; Conte didn't sign because she refused to underwrite a clause that made her jointly liable for Huffy's losses due to breach of contract or insurance claims. Thus, in a matter of hours the deal collapsed and the two riders were left without a bike sponsor.

Away from the business end of the sport, however, Johnson was riding, quite literally, like a pro. In 1988 he won the Pro Ramp Division at the World BMX Freestyle Championships in Manchester, England. Impressive performances in the 2Hip King of Vert series, where he consistently placed within the top three, positioned the free agent among the elite of the international freestyle scene. But perhaps his most significant contribution to the sport would be a moment of pure innovation, a moment that would continue to resonate through the sport for many years to come.

During the third round of the 1984 King of the Skate Parks Series, in Upland, California, Haro rider Mike Dominguez debuted a new trick. The Tail-Whip Fly-Out was an airborne version of a ground trick that had been invented two years earlier by Brian Blyther, also a Haro rider. The trick, which represented a new level of creativity within the sport, became a major talking point among riders who wanted to know where the sport could go next. In early 1988, Joe Johnson began working on an answer to that question when an unscheduled break in a European tour found him and Dennis McCoy with some downtime, in a hangar, with a 10-foot quarter-pipe to play with. A frustrating day of rotating the bike, under the coping, achieved little—but more experimentation on his back yard half-pipe after the tour convinced Johnson that it was physically possible. The breakthrough came in mid-August of 1988 when he achieved full rotation on his back-yard ramp and managed to get one foot on the pedal and the other on the frame before landing and rolling out.

Later that month, at the AFA Masters contest, in Wayne, New Jersey, Joe Johnson broke the future of BMX freestyle wide open. Having struggled to pull the new trick in practice, he persevered, and in front of a packed crowd of spectators and fellow riders he captured the moment and landed the first Tail-Whip Air ever seen in competition. He went on to perfect the trick at height and began pulling doubles in contests a year later.

A deal to ride for GT in the late 1980s became Joe Johnson's swan song as a professional BMX rider. With an eye to the future, in 1991 he returned to school full-time to study engineering. Today he lives in Massachusetts and occasionally rolls out on his bike. But he leaves his legacy, the Tail-Whip Air, for the new breed of freestyle riders to enjoy.

As Street riding emerged, so did the new possibilities. A "mulleted" Johnson jumps a AMC Pacer in Leucadia, CA - 1988.

A lot of guys were negotiating their deals and a lot of them didn't happen. I did speak with Bill [Hawkins] on a few occasions, and the deal Haro offered was incredible, but we had agreements with other sponsors and I wanted to honor that. Haro was starting to shake riders at the time because the economy of the sport was beginning to tank. It was a tough time for everybody and we just had to keep going and feel confident that something else would turn up.

- Joe Johnson

I started riding, as in jumping and pulling wheelies, back in 1971 in Arizona. Some older guys took me under their wing and took me to their trails close to where I lived. There was a path with some small jumps and a wooden launch. It was a fun time and place to be a young kid with a bike. When we moved back to Davenport I brought the BMX bug back with me. I became a sort of neighborhood Wheelie King…pretty much a young kid with no guidance, running wild on my bike.

– Rick Moliterno

The "Rope Aroni" at the AFA Masters contest Ohio, September 1988.

Palmetto Florida AFA Masters - January 1988. Moliterno rides to "Dude Looks Like a Lady" on his Professional debut.

Haro Tour of Kings 1988.

11 | RICK MOLITERNO

Rick Moliterno's phenomenal journey in BMX began when he was just 5 years old. In 1970, his family had left the Midwest town of Davenport, Iowa, for Apache Junction (a city situated east of Phoenix, Arizona). The change in location sealed young Rick's destiny when, soon after arriving in Arizona, he received a Spider––a chopper-style bicycle purchased from the local Sears. The purple banana seat and knobby tires were all he needed to begin a lifelong adventure on two wheels. By the time he was 10, the independence and opportunity provided by this first bike had forged an early lifestyle based on long hours of riding and experimenting with friends on the local trails. There was no set agenda: the long, sunny Southwestern days revolved around simply pedaling as fast and jumping as far and as high as possible. When the family returned to their hometown of Davenport in 1975, Moliterno continued where he had left off in Arizona: riding and experimenting on his bike in every spare moment he could find.

In 1979, at age 14, Moliterno entered a local ABA-sanctioned BMX race. With this first taste of organized racing, he relished the intensity and knew he had found his calling. In 1980, he won his first trophy at the Hawkeye BMX Raceway in Iowa City and the next three years of impressive results saw the teenage Moliterno swiftly rise through the amateur ranks of the ABA. In November of 1982, the ultimate moment arrived when he went to the Hawkeye Down's indoor BMX track in Cedar Rapids with a group of friends and equally committed racers to step up into the pro ranks of the ABA. During the next five years of white-knuckle racing, he would rise to eleventh place in the national ABA pro ranks.

Away from the track, in the summer of 1983, a creative alternative to BMX racing arrived in the Midwest in the form of the early Haro Freestyle tours. Bob Haro spent the first part the decade, which were also the early years of the

"Bottom side Candy Bar", Tour of Kings 1988.

experimental freestyle scene, engaging the youth of the country face to face by touring with his team and popularizing the Haro brand. That summer Haro visited Elkhart, Indiana with team rider Ron Wilton to perform a freestyle show at Bud's BMX, a local shop with a large BMX-hungry clientele. The arrival of the two freestylers further energized the regional scene and launched a period of ramp construction and experimentation among a thriving group of committed locals.

But it was in the summer of 1984, during Moliterno's fifth summer-racing season, that a pivotal opportunity arrived. With the blessing of Bike'n'Hike's owner, Rick had booked the newly formed GT factory freestyle team of Ron Wilkerson and Rich Avella to perform a show at the shop. For their part, Wilkerson and Avella had joined GT to tour the country to promote the brand and its new freestyle bike, the GT Performer. After the show, the two riders stayed in town to relax and ride with the locals for a couple of days. When Wilkerson offered Moliterno a seat in the truck on their day of departure, he packed a bag, grabbed his bike, and set off on a two-week journey around the Midwest.

I worked at Bike'n'Hike in Rock Island and they were my sponsors. The support of the owner there may have been the single biggest boost to helping me develop and pursue my riding to its full potential; in fact, I may have taken a different path without it. They helped with entry fees, bikes, and parts, and they also allowed me to bring in the GT and Haro freestyle teams for shows.

– Rick Moliterno

My friend Barry Ream and I built a quarter-pipe in around 1983. It was a pretty dubious-looking ramp, standing at around 9 feet tall with way too much vert. Before it separated from racing, freestyle was just what we did off the track. But after seeing the early Haro shows, we took it a step further. We wanted to see where we could take it and we just focused more on riding the ramp and street.

– Rick Moliterno

That sealed it for me. I built a dedicated freestyle bike after that GT tour and began to focus on freestyle riding. I continued racing until the end of '85, but freestyle was taking over and I just got hooked.

– Rick Moliterno

The summer of 1985 brought two more of the sport's top riders to the region when the Hutch Hi-Performance Freestyle Team arrived in the town of Cologne, Illinois. Moliterno had dedicated most of that year beyond the GT tour to improving his freestyle ability, so the

Stretched out "One hand, one footer" on the Haro Rampage Tour in 1987.

appearance of Woody Itson and Donovan Ritter presented a golden opportunity. Moliterno took his chance to impress the two Hutch riders and made an immediate impact. Within a few weeks, a new Hutch Trick Star frame and fork arrived in Davenport, courtesy of the brand, and two months later an invitation to tour with the teamcame via a telephone call from Woody Itson. Hutch needed a capable young rider to tour with Woody, due to the imminent departure of young vert specialist Mike Dominguez (to rival brand Diamond Back) after the development of some irreconcilable issues between the

young Californian and Randy Bowser, Hutch's notoriously outspoken tour manager. Moliterno rolled into action on the fall leg of the Hutch tour and held his own. Sadly, the Hutch arrangement would come to an abrupt end when the company filed for Chapter 11 bankruptcy in the late summer of 1986––a move that left both Itson and Moliterno without sponsorship. But still another opportunity, a career-defining one for Rick Moliterno, would soon be revealed.

Hutch pretty much died after the summer tour in 1986 and Woody and I rode for Rockville at the Nassau Island AFA contest. I stayed with the Haro crew and the crazy thing is that in 1985, both Hutch and Haro both called me within a few hours of each other to ride for them. Hutch had called earlier, and I had already accepted their offer to ride for them. But then I guess I ended up where I was supposed to be all along.

– Rick Moliterno

Moliterno would not remain a free agent for long: Hutch's ultimate decline became Haro's good fortune. Following numerous excellent performances in all disciplines, through a series of AFA contests Rick was becoming one of the most-talked-about young riders in the international freestyle scene. With his deep connections to the Haro freestyle team through friends Joe Johnson and Dennis McCoy, it seemed likely that an opportunity to ride for Haro was just around the corner. Moliterno had relocated to Kansas City in early '86 to manage a local bike shop while continuing to tour and compete for Hutch as an amateur. He found the

thriving scene in Kansas not only a perfect environment for experimentation, but also a great place to ride and network with some of the country's best and most innovative street riders

Rick was on Hutch, touring and competing as an amateur. He moved to Kansas City and we rode flatland together almost every night for a stretch. He seemed a logical choice for the team to me. I had spoken with Bill Hawkins and Jim Ford about the fact that Haro should sign him, but when Hutch went down he got the deal on his own ability amd merits.

– Dennis McCoy

Rick Moliterno officially joined the Haro Freestyle Team in September of 1986 and two months later rolled into his debut at the fifth round of the AFA Masters Series, in Dothan, Alabama, in the Sixteen and Over Expert Division. Within a month he was competing for Haro in the premier event of the year, the AFA Masters finals at the Velodrome, near Los Angeles. Although he placed a respectable fourth in the Competitive Flatland Division, he also performed well in vert and took the overall title for the day. The following year he waged a campaign of almost total flatland domination at contest level, having stepped up to compete in the Nineteen and Over Expert category. First place at the first round of the West Palm Beach AFA Masters in January was followed by three more victories: at Portland, Oregon; Austin, Texas; and Columbus, Ohio over stiff competition from East Coast prodigy Kevin Jones and GT's Dino DeLuca. The year 1987 had been a successful one for the

A "Rope Aroni" 1988 Tour of Kings somewhere in the Mid West.

The shows were high energy and we pushed each other in every one of them—in the best way. We had an unbelievable summer we all just wanted to ride our best and we were three people who got on really well together so it brought the best out of the situation.

The last AFA contest I entered is probably my favourite memory of that year. I won Pro Flat, and got second on ramps to Dennis. I was fortunate enough to have a lot of good luck in contests.

We opened Rampage for purely selfish reasons. A buddy and I wanted an indoor place to ride so we could build our own scene. The riders and riding were forcing the changes. Street and park were new and the learning curve was fat. Guys like Wilkerson and the Meet the Street Jams, and the Hoffman crew along with the Rampage/standard crew all had a hand in driving it forward in those days. But there was a huge list of others too.

– Rick Moliterno

young amateur, who walked away from his second full season of AFA competition with consecutive flatland and overall titles, as well as notoriety as a rising talent.

In the summer of 1987, Rick headed out on behalf of his new sponsor on what would become the most prosperous and well-attended tours of the early freestyle era. Along with teammates Dennis McCoy and Joe Johnson, and Australian announcer Nick Jonze, the team rolled out of Kansas City and headed east toward Michigan before blazing a trail through a series of Midwestern strongholds and on to the East Coast. Tours always produced interesting moments, and long nighttime riding sessions through the streets of Manhattan are remembered fondly by both Moliterno and McCoy, who regularly raised a group of locals to ride the city streets until the early-morning hours.

An opportunity to become the senior member of a summer touring team came in 1988, when Team Manager and Announcer Ron Haro joined Rick and two new young faces on the Tour of Kings. East Coast flatlander Joe Gruttola, and Mat Hoffman, an innovative young ramp rider from Oklahoma, represented the new breed of specialist rider that was regularly emerging out of the national contest scene, and the three formed a unit that expertly covered all aspects of freestyle riding. Hoffman's brief departure from the team the following year brought together new Haro recruit Lee Reynolds with Gruttola and Moliterno for the 1989 summer Tour of Kings.

If 1987 demonstrated Moliterno's potential as a great flatland rider, 1988 would become the year he staked his claim as a contender among the elite of the sport. The decision to step into the pro ranks not only pitched him against his good friend Dennis McCoy, it also gave him a chance to show the watching world that he could compete head to head with any rider in the world. The pro vert ranks contained a wealth of talent. Specialists, including Diamond Back's Mike Dominguez, GT's Josh White, and Haro's Brian Blyther, were all at the top of their game. Talented all-rounders including Ron Wilkerson, Dennis Langlais, and Dennis McCoy were also more than capable of winning any contest on any given day. This year, 1988, would prove to be a pivotal 12 months in the early history of the sport––and, ultimately, the last for the vert category within the AFA series of events.

The decline of the BMX business in 1989 took an inevitable toll on core of the sport. The AFA saw contest attendances fall, and this decline would eventually spell the end of the organization as a national leader in, and facilitator of, the freestyle contest scene. In response to the lack of organized contests, a number of senior riders created new and unique riding environments that in time would also serve as contest venues. In 1989, Moliterno and a close friend opened the Rampage Skate Park in Rick's hometown of Davenport. Although he would continue to ride, and be sponsored by Haro until early 1991, a lack of summer tours and contests would ultimately dilute and dissolve the relationships between the bike companies and many of the sport's top riders.

Rick Moliterno's place in history is assured as one of the greatest all-around BMX freestyle riders of all time. His wider contributions to the sport as an innovative rider, entrepreneur, sponsor, bike builder, contest facilitator, and ramp architect all helped the freestyle movement to grow and progress through some of its most famous highs and infamous lows. The sometimes-unbelievable moments of skill and innovation that he demonstrated on his bike through the 1980s and 1990s were not only inspiring to many, but also, more importantly, served to energize and introduce untold numbers of new riders to the phenomenal sport of BMX freestyle. And his legacy and commitment to the sport lives on. In 1991 Moliterno founded the Standard Bicycle Company, a BMX frame and fork manufacturing brand located in Davenport, Iowa. Standard continues to provide high quality, US-made custom BMX frame-and-fork sets to the core of the modern BMX race and freestyle scenes.

In the beginning, we were all just poor-ass street rats who would take every inch we could. Single-parent kids raising ourselves on our bikes and doing something that we loved every day.

– Rick Moliterno

Clicked look back on the 1987 Haro Rampage Tour.

We pulled up and parked the car. I opened the door to be confronted by Dennis McCoy doing a G-Turn in the parking lot. There was a jam circle forming up and it just immediately blew my mind. I hadn't really seen tricks like that and I literally couldn't believe what I was seeing.

– Joe Gruttola

"Front yard" on a 1988 blue Haro Master. 1988 Tour of Kings.

12 | JOE GRUTTOLA

In late December of 1985, the National Guard Armory, on the banks of the Merrimack River in Manchester, New Hampshire, played host to the first AFA Masters Freestyle Finals to be staged outside of California. The significance of both the event and its location would be realized in the months that followed, and as the nation's best freestyle riders descended on the town, the first truly national contest of the AFA's tenure began. Fourteen-year-old Joe Gruttola, who had been waiting for this moment, had a hunch that the weekend would be pivotal for his freestyle ambitions. Accompanied by his friend Jim Johnson, and Johnson's family, the group set off on the 540-mile round trip from their home town of Ronkonkoma in Long Island, New York. From the moment they arrived, the action came thick and fast.

Joe Gruttola's first encounter with freestyle came via his neighborhood friend George Gallo and a group of local kids in his hometown. The early 1980s saw a multitude of young BMX racers migrate to freestyle in the wake of magazine coverage that promoted this creative, street-based alternative to racing. Gruttola himself had raced for a short period, but the appearance of neighborhood kids experimenting on their bikes became a distraction. Young Joe quickly became obsessed by the creative challenge, dropping anchor in the driveway of the family home for hours at a time as he ventured into the all-absorbing challenge of freestyle BMX.

I got my first bike—a chrome Schwinn Predator—when I was 11 years old. I took a road trip with my dad to Ohio, where I found a copy of Super BMX in a store. Not long after, a couple of kids in my neighborhood appeared riding around on bikes with Skyway Tuff wheels. I kept seeing these guys rolling around the neighborhood doing tricks and they actually built a pretty decent quarter-pipe too. At the time it was the only one Long Island, so I decided I would keep my own company and concentrate on riding flat.

-Joe Gruttola

Returning energized and completely blown away by what he had witnessed at the AFA Finals, Joe decided that to realize his ambitions, as well as to break into the national scene, he needed a plan. The first step involved mail ordering a VHS copy of the Manchester event, which enabled him to study the techniques of accomplished senior riders like McCoy, Dennis Langlais, Martin Aparijo, Chris Lashua, and Ron Wilkerson. As soon as the mail carrier pushed the rectangular package into the family mailbox, Gruttola's weekends and evenings began to revolve around long hours in front of the TV as he freeze-framed, memorized, visualized, and reverse-engineered the tricks. Every daytime minute he could spare was devoted to setting up and experimenting on his bike in the family driveway. As he hit one milestone of progress after another and his confidence grew, he began to test himself by entering a series of local AFA contests that were being staged in National Guard armories and schoolyards in the greater Massachusetts area.

Repping a 2Hip tee-shirt for a magazine shoot in 1987.

Leaned over "Front yard", 1987.

In the Summer of 1987, Gruttola headed to Woodward East Camp in Pennsylvania to teach Freestyle riding.

I set my sights on learning the hardest and scariest trick I could find in the magazines, and that was a creation of Woody Itson's that he called the Bar Ride. I spent the summer trying to develop an original trick and I decided I was going to practice the Bar Ride, but I would face backwards because nobody had done it that way yet. I knew that if I was going to stand out, I had to do something more than just the known tricks; I needed something that I could truly call my own invention that would give me an edge. It took me six months but I got it really dialed in. I decided if I was going to make an impact, I needed to try to get to California where the scene was blowing up. I dreamed of pulling the trick for the first time at a national contest.

– Joe Gruttola

When I had a few tricks down, I started competing in some local contests that were sponsored by the Boy Scouts at the armories, but I quickly realized that I didn't feel quite ready and decided to just practice more. I was 14 at the time and it occurred to me that to get where I really wanted to be, I needed a plan. I looked at the age groups and identified the guys I would be competing with if I could break into the National AFA ranks; guys like Scotty Freeman and Brain Belcher. I also knew that I needed a certain amount of known tricks, but also a couple of original tricks of my own. I practiced relentlessly for a year, literally spending almost every spare moment outside of school on my bike. When I felt ready, I started to compete at local level again.

- Joe Gruttola

Gruttola's re-entry into the contest scene in early 1986 paid off almost immediately. His almost-scientific approach to improlatland skills had prepared him to rejoin the AFA armory scene as a much better rider, with an arsenal of more-refined tricks and the confidence to compete in front of a crowd. Within a few months he caught the eye of SE Racing's Perry Kramer. Kramer immediately recognized the teenager's obvious talent and arranged for Joe to begin representing SE via a connection with the local Farmingdale's bike shop. The arrangement provided Joe with a bike (an SE Racing Trickmaster), a uniform, and a commitment to run a series of weekend clinics at the bike shop with his friend George Gallo aimed at helping other local youngsters get started in freestyle. But it was in the winter of 1986 that 15-year-old Joe Gruttola would transcend the local scene and take his destiny into his own hands.

Joe sat down with his father to reveal his elaborate plan, which revolved around a key date in the AFA freestyle contest calendar and a trip to the other side of the country. In November of 1986, the best of the national AFA freestyle ranks would form up at the Dominguez Hills Velodrome in Compton, a neighborhood in South Central Los Angeles, for the premier event of the year: the AFA Masters Finals. Gruttola had remained in contact with a high-school friend, Scotty Ewing, who had relocated to San Diego from Long Island with his family the year before. Scotty's family offered Joe a place to stay if he was able to make the trip; first, however, he would need to make his own way to the West Coast––with his bike. In recognition of his son's commitment and belief, Joe's father was satisfied that he would be in safe hands and agreed that the trip did indeed represent a golden opportunity. So in November, along with his friends Tom Gentile and Joe Oliva, Gruttola headed to the Islip MacArthur Airport on Long Island, with his bike and a bag of clothes, to embark upon the journey that would truly redefine his future.

The Velodrome wasn't just a freestyle contest to me: it was California! Land of warm winters, earthquakes, movie stars, and the home of something that I truly loved: BMX freestyle. Arriving at the contest arena was intimidating; I wasn't as put together as Scotty Freeman, or as smooth as Martin [Aparijo], but those guys were my inspiration. When I got my chance, I felt like I pulled the perfect routine, including the first backwards Bar Ride and backwards Decade ever seen in a contest. The magazines shot some photographs and published them with the caption 'Who is this guy?' I was almost completely unknown, and I won the 14/15 Expert Flatland category on my debut.

– Joe Gruttola

The impact of Gruttola's appearance and performance at the Velodrome would kick-start a series of events that would bring him face to face with a pioneer and legend of the sport. Bob Haro had watched Joe's run with interest and wanted to find out how this talented East Coaster had made it to the national freestyle arena almost completely under the radar. As the dust settled, Joe returned to San Diego and spent the remainder of the weekend riding at Mission Bay with a group of locals. Among the group was Jon Peterson, a former Skyway team manager and skate-park rider who had worked for Bob Haro in the company's formative years as a show announcer, team rider, and team manager.

Two days after the contest, I was riding with some locals and I first met Jon Peterson. He came over to me and started talking about some guy who had pulled a Backwards Bar Ride at the Velodrome contest and nobody knew who he was. I said, 'That was me,' and he told me that Bob Haro wanted to meet me. Then he drove me directly to the Haro offices in Carlsbad, where I met with Bob and he offered me a deal. I was choked up and nervous but it felt like something was going my way. I was on SE at the time and it didn't sit well to make a decision without telling them so I called them from the office and explained

At home in Long Island, 1986. Gruttola celebrates a local AFA win with a "Cherry picker."

what had happened. They understood. It was Haro! Bob gave me a bike and a uniform and said he wanted to send me to Florida for the AFA contest the following February and if I did well, we could work out a better deal.

– Joe Gruttola

The 1987 AFA series opener in West Palm Beach, Florida, was a mouth-watering prospect for Joe Gruttola. Motivated by the promise of a full factory deal on what was arguably the team of the decade, he didn't disappoint. Meeting stiff competition from Skyway's Scott Freeman and General's Brian Belcher, in the words of the BMX press, Gruttola "slaughtered the class" with a run full of innovative and well-executed tricks, including the Backwards Bar Ride and a No-Handed Backward Infinity Roll complete with

Haro Tour of Kings 1988 - "G-turn, one handed bottle rocket" Gruttola in groundbreaking form for the kids and his sponsor

Spinning Bars. Confidence was high after the victory, but a baptism of fire back at the team hotel soon put everything into perspective.

Victory in Palm Beach opened the door to a whole new world of opportunities. Bob Haro kept his word, and team manager Bill Hawkins would nurture Joe's development as he signed on to become a full factory Haro rider. His first summer was spent working as a freestyle instructor at the Woodward East Summer camp in Pennsylvania with a group of other young riders that included Hutch's Rick Allison and Schwinn's Robert Peterson. A series of freestyle shows in front of the young campers provided daily opportunities to practice and refine tricks. Time off was usually spent working out; Joe would leave the camp the end of the summer in the best shape of his life. In September, he arrived at Round 4 of the

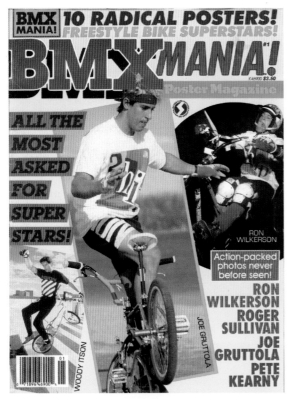

The accolade of a magazine cover in the most populated era of the sport was an achievement.

AFA Masters Series in Columbus, Ohio, having moved up to the 16–18 Expert category, and once again showed his class by taking second place and narrowly missing out on first to Mongoose rider Karl Rothe. Victory in Wayne, New Jersey, in October, brought more new tricks and innovation. The double whip-lash and the ground breaking "Hang Five" formed part of a more confident evolved routine and both tricks had emerged from a period of intense experimentation that also brought Gruttola third place at the AFA finals in Carson, in November.

The year 1988 got started in the best possible way. A repeat of his previous Round One victory at the AFA Masters opener in Florida set the tone for a year that would bring the teenager further into the national spotlight. The numerous opportunities that came with the Haro deal were almost unbelievable, although the disadvantage of living almost 3000 miles away from the company's head office would become a frustration. A solution to this problem began, once again, with a negotiation between Joe and his parents.

I remember meeting the other team riders at the hotel, and it was chaos. I manage to piss-off Rick Moliterno immediately, I had that effect on people. He threw a handle bar stem at me, which stuck in the wall just above my head. This was also the weekend of the infamous "Large Ray" microwave incident, when every rider from every team got thrown out of the hotel and told never to return under any circumstances. It was quite a view seeing 200 plus riders and team managers walking across the freeway to another hotel.

– Joe Gruttola

The way things were developing; In my opinion it made sense for me to be in California. I agreed to some conditions with my parents. Basically that I would sign myself out of school for six months and make the move, but I would finish my studies—and I did. They were obviously concerned, but they knew how important my career was and they allowed me to move to the Enchanted house in Leucadia to live with Kevin [Martin] and a group of other riders. During that period we filmed the Team Haro movie, agro riding and Kung Fu fighting with Eddie Roman and a how-to trick video for BMX Plus! Called 101 Freestyle Tricks. And then in the summer, I got to head out on the Tour of Kings with Mat [Hoffman], Rhino, and Rick [Moliterno].

– Joe Gruttola

The 1988 Tour of Kings was a baptism of fire for both Hoffman and Gruttola. Both riders had opted to take a break from school to purse their BMX ambitions, and neither had traveled extensively. Senior team rider Rick Moliterno and team manager/announcer Ron "Rhino" Haro were charged with making responsible decisions and getting the tour successfully through its three-month schedule. Nonetheless, the two teenagers would quickly learn to grow up and take care of themselves on this unrelenting cross-country trek.

I have vivid memories of scraping gravel out of Hoffman's hands and then basically watching him duct-tape himself back together to continue riding in a show. Mat was always really humble and a good friend to me and on that tour I felt completely at one with my bike. We constantly thought about new tricks and how we could improve them; it was always a case of doing your best for the kids who made the effort to come out and see us. On more than one occasion I gave my bike away after a show. There would always be a few kids without bikes and I always felt that they needed the one I had more than I did. This would usually upset the guys back at Haro though. They would get invoices from the bike shops because I would just build a bike out of their inventory when we arrived at the next show.

– Joe Gruttola

The next year, 1989, would become Joe Gruttola's final year as a sponsored rider in the professional freestyle scene. With the industry spiraling into a steep decline and the demise of the AFA, opportunities to compete in the flatland arena were becoming limited to a series of low-key, one-off events at random hot spots around the country. However, the technical skills that had served him well in his flatland development would transition well into the emerging and dominant street scene. The 2Hip Meet the Street series quickly became the premier event on the contest calendar. The events were raw, innovative, and experimental––true representations of the evolution of the freestyle scene and its almost full-circle return to its pure roots.

I was more of a mini-ramp guy than a vert rider. I took a technical approach to street, probably due to being a flatlander and being focused on trying to be smooth. But I loved the freedom of street riding and was one of a few guys early on who could pull a great wall ride from flat. What Bob Haro did for this sport became a life-changing experience for me. He was a guy who just went for something, and among all of the guys out there riding fast, jumping, and trying to work out what this was, Bob was experimenting, visualizing, and creating something truly amazing.

- Joe Gruttola

"Fast plant" at the Brooklyn Banks in New York. Circa 1988 or 1989.

The slow shutter speed captures the full sequence of a "Look Back" on the backyard Half pipe in Catonsville, Maryland.

The youngest of four brothers, Jeremy Alder was born and raised in the town of Catonsville, a leafy suburb west of Baltimore, Maryland. His early ambitions to ride and own a BMX bike led him to Pete's Cycles, a neighborhood bike shop in Baltimore where he and his friends would often peer through the window at the rows of Mongoose and GT BMXes, occasionally venturing inside to leaf through the magazines and catalogues that lined the shelves. It was through these community shops and the industrious early BMX press that the formative freestyle brands would reach out and inspire their captive young audience to pick up a bike and ride. Jeremy Alder needed little encouragement to indulge his instincts, however. Through the mid-1980s he would rise through the ranks of the NFA and AFA contest scene to secure a place on the late-1980s Haro Factory Freestyle team.

The early years in Catonsville passed in a blur of dirt jumping and experimentation that saw the four brothers and a group of local friends obsessively forge and refine their bike skills on a series of jumps and ramps in their neighborhood. The discovery of a half-pipe, built by a group of local skaters in some nearby woodland, provided their first opportunity to ride vert. Twelve-year-old Jeremy would be the first to rise to the challenge and find his calling.

When I first started riding, my influences were my brothers. All I wanted to do was jump and get as good as they were. There was an Ocean Pacific advertisement in BMX Action that showed Bob Haro doing an

Air on a plexiglass quarter-pipe, and it just blew me away. I remember thinking that on a ramp like that I could go as high as I wanted and land smooth…and maybe stop breaking bike parts. From that moment on I just wanted to ride a quarter-pipe. I got my first bike for Christmas in 1982, and although my jumping and riding improved, by the end of '83 I had broken the frame twice. I got a third frame on the warranty scheme, but I decided to sell it to raise money for something better suited to freestyle riding. Through the fall and winter of '83, I took odd jobs from friends and neighbors, borrowing a bike wherever I could. Then in the spring of '84, I bought the new GT Performer frame and fork.

– Jeremy Alder

The year 1984 would be decisive for 13-year-old Jeremy Alder. The local crew in Catonsville had continued to relentlessly indulge their passion for the new sport; by the summer, a new addition in the form of a 6-foot quarter-pipe stood in the yard of the Alder family home. The ramp offered convenience and independence that would steer Jeremy onto a steep learning curve and accelerate his progression. In June, the ultimate inspiration arrived with the launch of Freestylin', a magazine dedicated to the developing freestyle scene that had now truly separated from its roots in BMX racing. With a modest array of tricks, Alder teamed up with a friend and flatland rider named Jon Mueller to form the AM (Alder/Mueller) trick team.

The summer of 1984 was when freestyle really took off. I was saving for a new frame and fork and didn't have a bike for months so I would borrow my brothers' or friend's bikes whenever I could while I worked jobs to save up for a new frame and fork. We built a six-and-a-half-foot quarter-pipe at a friend's house, but like our ramp-riding skills at the time, the construction was pretty sketchy. Some of the local parents felt it was too dangerous so we moved it and then eventually built our own at home. That summer my friend John Mueller and I decided to start a trick team that we named after ourselves. We got sponsorship from a local pub and a restaurant that paid for some jerseys and local contest entries.

– Jeremy Alder

In April of 1985, a freestyle show at a local BMX track brought to town two of California's rising stars, Hutch's Mike Dominguez and Woody Itson. The Hutch Hi-Performance brand was a unique proposition. Founded by local entrepreneur Richard Hutchins in Maryland in 1979, Hutch began as a BMX mail-order company before Hutchins recognized the opportunity to develop proprietary products for the BMX racing scene. The brand would attract some of the best racers and freestyle riders of the era, and Hutchins would go on to found the National Freestyle Association, which played an important role in legitimizing freestyle in the Southeast United States.

.Shortly after the Hutch demo, Alder entered his first local freestyle contest; demonstrating the potential that would set him on the path to even greater success, he took first place.

Jeremy "Inverts" one footed on the Backyard Quarter in Catonsville.

It was always my dream to be sponsored by a factory team. As soon as I started riding freestyle, I knew I wanted to be as good as I could be. I simply loved the sport. I won a couple of local contests in '84 and then in 1985, we all started competing in the NFA contests centered on Maryland and Virginia. I worked really hard to learn new tricks and I continued to improve; I won all nine events between September and December. When the organization folded in the summer of 1986, I was the NFA 14–15 Expert Ramp Champion. (Brother) Joe and I turned to the AFA so we could continue to compete but we had no support, so travel costs and replacement parts were all down to us. I It wasn't easy to compete on a regular basis.

– Jeremy Alder

As the freestyle movement erupted out of California and locked into its global audience, 1985 saw the floodgates open. A packed summer tour schedule brought the factory freestyle teams deep into fan communities, where large crowds flocked to local venues to see the magazine stars up close. Rockville BMX, a dedicated BMX and skate shop located 35 miles east of Catonsville, became a mecca for the East Coast scene through the rest of the decade. Almost every brand with its own factory team would pass through the town, performing shows for thousands of young fans. GT's Eddie Fiola, Dave Breed, Rick Allison, and Martin Aparijo arrived at Rockville in early July, with RL Osborn and Ron Wilton from the BMX Action Trick Team and the legendary Haro team of Ron Wilkerson, Brian Blyther, and Dave Nourie following later in the month. This intense period of activity energized locals and amplified the call for regulated amateur events—a call answered by the formation of the NFA in the late summer of 1985. Although the organization would be indirectly absorbed by the American Bicycle Association within a year, the facilitation of a series of contests over that 12-month period would nurture and grow regional participation in the sport.

The next 12 months would bring Jeremy Alder into contention within the national ranks of the American Freestyle Association's Masters Series. With a range of tricks that included No-Footer-One-Handers, Topside No-Foot-Can-Cans and Airs at 7 feet out, he transitioned seamlessly from the NFL to the AFA. After attending an AFA event at Madison Square Garden in June of '86 as a spectator, Alder decided he was ready to step into the national contest arena. His debut at the fourth round of the AFA Masters at New York's Nassau Community College in late

September pitted him against Skyway's young vert prodigy, Mat Hoffman. A confident run with smooth variations brought him second place in New York, and he would see out the 1986 contest season with victories at a series of local AFA contests in Maryland.

With the start of the AFA season on February 1 in West Palm Beach, Florida, 1987 became the year that Jeremy Alder's ramp tricks gained him genuine recognition and wider opportunities. First he took fourth place in a 14–15 Expert Ramp Division that was packed with young international talent. Limited by a lack resources to fund travel and contest overheads, he continued to evolve and refine a range of tricks through the spring and early summer while also attending and networking with riders at some of the Haro Freestyle Tour shows that came through Maryland. Friendships with Rick Moliterno, Dennis McCoy, and Joe Johnson would help Jeremy evolve even further and gain even more positive coverage.

I had heard that Hutch was looking for riders. I lived down the street from the company offices. They had recently hired Ron Stebenne [an AFA affiliate promoter from Massachusetts] to build a team for them. I called them directly and they told me to call Ron—who, since he didn't know anything about me, sent me a contract to ride for a probationary period. Later that evening, before I went to the post office, Bill Hawkins called and asked if either Joe or myself was sponsored. I did have a contract with Hutch, but I hadn't mailed it back to Ron yet. Bill, as Haro team manager, told me what Haro would be prepared to offer us; not only was it way better than Hutch, I was already riding a Haro Sport—I loved it and it was my first choice of frame. I was so excited that the following day I actually called Bill at Haro and asked if the offer was for real! I must have sounded a little strange.

Words cannot express the emotion of becoming sponsored, and on top of that it was Haro, which was unbelievable! In September a box arrived,with jerseys, race pants, gloves, stickers, mouth guards, elbow guards…we were blown away. In November, the new 1988 Haro bike range came out and they called and asked us what specific models and colors we wanted. I remember coming home from school and sitting in my living room looking at two boxes, both with 'Haro Freestyler' printed across them. I took the box that said 'Sport,' laid the box on its side, and literally laid my body on top the box and stayed there face down.

– Jeremy Alder

The opportunity to join Haro was not only exciting; it presented itself during a period when Alder was at his most creative as a rider. In the fall of '87 he improvised and invented the 360 Abubaca. Now regularly pushing 9 feet of air and pulling 540s four to five feet above coping, Alder would once again clear up in the closing months of '87 by entering and winning contests in Maryland and Pennsylvania before returning in Haro colors to the AFA season opener in Palmetto, Florida, in January of 1988 and placing second to Mat Hoffman. More improvisation followed, away from the contest arena. Later on, a week spent riding at the home of Rick Moliterno brought Jeremy closer to a defining moment in his career.

I had wanted to try a full 360 Bar Spin for a while after seeing pictures of Todd Anderson pulling a half in a magazine. We had been riding at Rick's house for a week and were discussing how to approach it. I knew that I probably wouldn't pull it the first try, so I thought about where the best place to attempt it would be. I figured the best place was on a smooth concrete surface, unlike the driveway at my house, which would really tear me up if I fell. The local AFA affiliate held

contests at Ann Arundel County Fairgrounds in Maryland and the concrete was very smooth. So I waited 'til that next contest and decided to try and get the bars all the way around. It was after the contest that I decided to attempt it. I crashed on my first and third attempts and pulled in on the second and fourth. Somebody was shooting video and a shot of the trick made it into the December '88 issue of Freestylin', in the Graffiti section.

– Jeremy Alder

In March, the AFA Masters Series drew the freestyle world to the Pacific Northwest, namely to the city of Portland, Oregon, where 16-year-old Jeremy claimed his first AFA victory as a Haro rider. The contest season was, as usual, punctuated by the summer tour window; this year, it offered new opportunities for both Joe and Jeremy to represent their sponsor away from the contest arena. Along with existing members of the Haro team, the brothers took part in a series of summer freestyle shows in the Southeastern US, including an appearance at Rockville BMX in Maryland. Second place in the AFA Masters in Wayne, New Jersey, in August was followed by another victory at Round 6 in Columbus, Ohio, where Jeremy would pull the first 360 Bar Spin in a national contest. An unfortunate head injury sustained before Round 7 of the Masters in Los Angeles led to Alder's only poor result of the year, but a month later he made off with first place at the Series Finals in Wichita, Kansas and won the season's overall vert title in the 17 Expert Ramp Division.

"Griz air" in practice for the 2Hip King of Vert, Newport Beach, CA.

Haro's support is what enabled me to develop and grow as a rider, as a competitor, and as a person. They gave me the opportunity to pursue my greatest passion with the best equipment, great people, and the freedom to express my creativity and live as the person I wanted to be.

– Jeremy Alder

The back-yard quarter pipe in Catonsville allowed Jeremy to push himself out of his comfort zone every day.

1988 was a great year for my career. I received my first bike from Haro in November of '87 and went to the January '88 AFA in Florida. I felt great pressure to perform and do well, so I rode even harder. I worked so hard, and it was paying off, and that motivated me to work even harder. I had great equipment, a new bike, new teammates, and I now had an opportunity to go to more of the AFA comps and do well. As the year unfolded, I felt confident and learned some new variations, but as a competitor I was still not at the level I wanted. I never had that perfect run that made me say, 'That was awesome.' In my class, Mat Hoffman was the guy to beat. Not only was he a fantastic rider, he was a good guy and always a friendly competitor. I never managed to beat him, but it was always fun trying.

– Jeremy Alder

Alder's first full year with Haro had been a great success. However, with the business end of the sport entering a worrying downturn in prosperity, the freestyle brands would soon take actions that would resonate throughout the sport. The AFA contest organization became one of the high-profile casualties of the year. The virtual collapse in the economy at the corporate end of the sport had taken its toll, and with attendances declining and costs rising, in 1989 those in power would decide to reinvent the format as a contest arena exclusively for flatland riders. The Alder brothers had a productive six months, however, during which they built a 10-foot-tall half pipe at home, filmed a follow-up to their BMX lifestyle movie, Alder Tricks, and riding in a series of regional freestyle shows for Haro at bike shops. Jeremy and his brother Joe would both leave Haro during August of 1989, as resources and support were withdrawn, but Jeremy Alder's two-year association with Haro Designs had already become the defining era of his early career in BMX freestyle.

Alder broke new ground in the sport when he pulled the first "Full Bar spin" at the Ann Arundel County Fair in Maryland, 1988.

Joe pulls a "Switch Footed front yard" sequence at home in Baltimore, 1988.

To reach the national ranks as a competitive flatland BMX rider in the late 1980s demanded levels of commitment and character that were often unrecognized. In an era when the evolution of freestyle had become intensely diverse, an inevitable point of divergence between vert and flatland riding began to direct the two evolved disciplines onto their own unique but separate paths. Specialist flatland and vert riders had both begun to emerge in the scene, which enabled the sport to evolve more rapidly. But this culture would also define the more complex challenges that lay ahead for the BMX industry as the decade rolled on.

Joe Alder grew up in the town of Catonsville, Maryland and spent his childhood riding and experimenting on bikes with his brothers and a group of neighborhood friends. His first encounter with a bicycle came in 1972 when he was just over 2 years of age. Joe received his first 20-inch bike for Christmas and with the aid of anybody that could help him mount up (since he couldn't touch the ground) he was mobile and able to experience the freedom that only a bicycle can offer. At the age of 11, he was jumping and bunny-hopping curbs on a spray-bombed Huffy; when he was 12, using the money he had saved from a series of part-time jobs, he purchased a Mongoose BMX.

In 1985, the steady increase in local freestyle contests in the Baltimore area created a series of opportunities for the growing band of local riders to showcase their abilities. In April, Joe looked on as his younger brother, Jeremy, won a ramp contest at a local BMX racetrack, and having witnessed the skills and abilities of the more-advanced riders, he left the track in a determined mood. Regular opportunities abounded to witness the sport's leading riders in action at local freestyle mecca, Rockville BMX, as the Californian factory teams funneled through the region on long summer tours. Exposure to the magazine stars and the exhilarating atmosphere of the Rockville shows convinced Joe to dedicate himself to learning and mastering the art of flatland riding.

That July, the hours of dedication and practice paid off. In his first contest, Joe delivered a skilled although slightly nervous routine that netted him his first step onto the podium and third place in his age group. This watershed contest experience turned into more opportunities for the 15-year-old as freestyle tightened its hypnotic grip on the youth of the country. Even better, the National Freestyle Association made its timely arrival thanks to Richard Hutchins, the founder and owner of the Hutch Hi-Performance BMX brand who founded the NFA late that summer. In September, Joe traveled to Rockville BMX for the NFA's debut contest. His nerves got the better of him and he placed disappointingly, but his work ethic would engender a reversal of fortune within months.

We began bunny-hopping and curb-jumping wherever we found an obstacle. Then my Mongoose got stolen and I bought a brand-new GT race bike with the insurance money. I was getting a little stronger and the bike was much lighter, so my jumping started to improve. We started going to a local BMX track to use the jumps to get air and then a few months later I took a brief detour into trying to learn to skateboard on ramps. Then when the Hutch Freestyle team of Woody Itson and Mike Dominguez came to our local BMX track, in early 1985, I felt that I could actually learn what we were seeing. I decided to give up organized team sports, put Skyways and pegs on my GT race bike, and began learning ground tricks with a group of locals.

Jeremy and I picked up sponsorship from Jerry Holland, a local BMX promoter who ran the racetrack and a small bike shop and later became the local AFA rep. From the beginning I started entering the contests in the Expert class, but for the first several contests, I placed third or fourth out of four or five riders. I believed in myself, though, and at year-end finals events [the Grand Nationals] in December, I was as strong a contender as anyone in my age group. After just six months of flatland riding, I placed second at the Grands, just behind a factory-sponsored rider from the Midwest. I also appeared in a magazine for the first time and signed my first autograph.

–Joe Alder

We used to watch contest and show footage on a daily basis, as a training tool to learn new tricks and perfect our form. We got the idea of taking all of our best footage and putting it together in one video for ourselves. We realized we could sell it when we saw that the first Dorkin' In York video was selling. In just a few months we sold about 200 copies through word of mouth.

– Joe Alder

The untimely demise of the NFA in December 1985 was an unsettling development for the freestyle faithful. However, in 1986, a local chapter of the American Freestyle Association was formed under the management of local promoter Jerry Holland. In February 1986, Joe entered and won first place in his AFA debut in Pennsylvania, beating local PA Factory rider Gary Pollak. Hoping to dedicate more time to riding and competing, Joe and Jeremy Alder both began to reach out for more sponsorship and support by preparing resumes that featured not only their riding skills but also their personalities and philosophies about BMX and its lifestyle. Even though they contacted a number of the known brands directly, due to the escalation and exposure the sport was receiving, the brothers were competing with thousands of other kids across the country who were keen to break into the national spotlight. Their appeals for support would have to wait a little while longer.

The next logical step for successful local competitors was the AFA Masters series. As a national contest network, the Masters included a pro class and had become the pinnacle of the competitive BMX contest scene. Although hampered by a lack of funding, Joe managed to travel to and compete in two national contests between September of 1987 and February of 1988. With numerous local AFA contests to keep him busy the rest of the time, a lifestyle of almost constant riding and experimenting ensued.

In the summer of 1987, freestyle BMX reached its zenith. An ambitious summer touring campaign brought the established factory freestyle brands out of their element and deep into the countryside with a single goal: to get more kids onto BMX bikes, which would help the companies to create more brand advocates.

Through their connection and friendship with Haro's Rick Moliterno, Joe Johnson, and Dennis McCoy, both Joe and Jeremy were offered opportunities to ride alongside their sponsored friends at a series of summer Haro Freestyle tour shows across the East and Midwest. This chance to ride in front of audiences in the company of three heavily connected pro riders led directly to an opportunity for the talent and commitment of the two brothers to shine.

A series of excellent results at the AFA Masters through the 1988 contest calendar demonstrated Joe Alder's evolution as a dedicated and innovative rider and fully justified his status and position on the Haro team. Next, back in Catonsville, the brothers began working on another freestyle-related project. Using some of the video footage they had shot of each other riding, with some guest appearances from a number of other factory riders, they produced a BMX lifestyle video titled Alder Tricks You Can Stand.

The year 1989 started with more promising opportunities for the young flatlander. In the spring, a photo shoot with Freestylin' magazine brought future Freestylin' magazine photographer Spike Jonze to Maryland and resulted in a two-page feature. A series of guest appearances on the 1989 Haro Tour of Kings in late July and early August brought the brothers together with Rick Moliterno, Lee Reynolds, Joe Gruttola, and Kevin Martin. A memorable show in front of hundreds of fans at Rockville was a high point, but within a month the brothers would become casualties of the infamous collapse of the freestyle market. Along with a high proportion of the era's factory-sponsored riders, they soon found themselves once again, financing their own freestyle lifestyle.

"Miami Hopper", Catonsville, 1986.

From spring of 1986 to the summer of 1987, I competed in AFA contests that were arranged and run by Jerry Holland in Maryland. I won around 50 percent of them and began meeting some of the bigger names in the sport, like Rick Moliterno (Haro) and Gary Pollak (CW), who were both at the NFA Grands in late '85. In April of 1987, Jeremy and I met Rick, Joe Johnson, and Dennis McCoy at a Dan-Up freestyle show and rode with them after the show. All of us became pretty good friends. We would often visit and ride with those guys for a week at a time.

– Joe Alder

Spinning a "Decade" on a 1987 Diamond Back Strike Zone.

Jamie Mills, Joe and Jeremy take a break.

The dream of breaking into the evolved and highly populated national BMX freestyle ranks in the late 1980s was a considerable challenge for any teenager––regardless of luck, location, or ability. But Joe and Jeremy Alder both recognized and rose to the occasion by demonstrating a unique level of focus and a commitment to the cause that would ultimately land them with the most exciting freestyle brand in the world.

We attended a series of Haro shows in the area and rode with Dennis, Rick, and Joe after the shows. I had a learned a few new tricks like the Locomotive and some spinning tricks, and I invented the Rolaid. This was probably the time when the guys decided to suggest recommending us to Haro. As you can imagine, the status of having a sponsor, not to mention the financial resources that came along with it, felt like quite an accomplishment for a 15-year-old who was used to pushing a lawn-mower for upgraded bike parts! I was extremely excited when the Haro team manager, Bill Hawkins, called to ask us if we would like to join the team. I felt a tremendous sense of having arrived at something, and at the same time needing to live up to something, so I was happy and a little anxious as well. I knew contests wouldn't be quite the same. On the local level, it gave me a huge amount of confidence and I rode better, no question. It also helped me deal with my nervousness and gave me greater focus. The other riders probably treated me a little differently too. It also made it easier to meet and get to know other kids; giving out an autograph here or there was kind of fun. At the national level, well, much of the confidence carried over and I clearly started performing much better. But at times I still felt pressure to be 'good enough to be sponsored.'

Being sponsored by Haro was empowering. I really wanted to promote the products and truly believed they were the best and most innovative company in the sport. Haro product sales, bikes, clothes, etc., must have peaked in the Baltimore/Washington DC area in 1988 and 1989. Almost everyone at the local contests was riding GTs before that, but most seemed to be riding Haros after we were sponsored. I always hoped Bob's investment in Jeremy and me paid dividends and made a difference somehow. I'm pretty sure it did.

– Joe Alder

Brian Blyther blasts a one footed, one handed Can-Can on the 1988
Tour of Kings. Wilkerson watches on from the deck.

15 | 1988 - 1990

GOOD TIMES, BAD TIMES

Haro Design's first 12 months under new ownership were a spectacular success. In spite of the wealth of new resources, investment, and distribution opportunities they had welcomed, Bob Haro and Jim Ford would declare that they hadn't deviated from their long-term plan. New ownership had undeniably presented new challenges, however. The company was now a component of a much larger organization, which meant that Haro and Ford's ability to effect change and move quickly within the fast-trending market was hindered by the bureaucracy of layered management and diminished responsibility.

Still, in December of 1987, it was hard to argue that the acquisition of Haro Designs had been anything but a resounding success for West Coast Cycle. The companies business had almost doubled in size within 12 months, with a more streamlined plan that curtailed the experimental foray into the skateboard scene in favor of renewed focus on the core BMX business and the booming mountain-bike market. However, 1988 would bring a change of fortune for the Haro management team. In September of 1988, the Raleigh Cycle Company of America (Huffy Corporation) and West Coast Cycle (Medalist Industries) merged to become the Derby Cycle Corporation. The move, which was orchestrated by West Coast Cycle President

Sid Dunofsky, immediately positioned Derby as the second largest supplier to the US specialty-bicycle market behind competitor Schwinn, and swept up the West Coast house brands of Nishiki, Cycle Pro and Haro into one gigantic brand portfolio. Dunofsky believed that by utilizing the apparently inexhaustible distribution resources of his former company, he could fast-track the Raleigh Worldwide brand into a favorable market position in the United States through the high-margin independent bicycle-dealer network. However, with the BMX market heading into the abyss and Raleigh failing to develop its adult business effectively, limitations on cash flow and resources began to take their toll.

Away from the numbers, a more personal negotiation was under discussion. After bursting onto the pro freestyle scene in early 1986, after encouragement to step up from the amateur ranks from Bob Haro and Jim Ford, Dennis McCoy's all-around ability and relentless appetite for all forms of competition had paid dividends for Haro. In 1987 he won the overall AFA pro freestyle title and the highly prized NORA Cup (Number One Rider Award), an honor voted on by the readers of Freestylin' magazine and a firm favorite of the riders. But as the year drew to a close, McCoy began to consider his options and future opportunities.

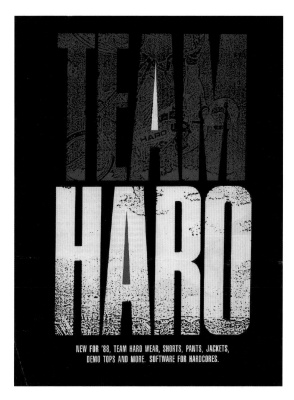

I had signed a long-term deal with Haro when I joined in late 1984 as an amateur. By 1988, I was one of the top pro riders in the country but was still on the same deal. I was earning a lot less than most of the other guys on the team, and most of the riders in the pro class, so I had to look at my options.

A discussion with fellow pro Eddie Fiola led to an introduction to freelance sports industry agent Micki Conte. Fiola had secured a lucrative contract to represent Levi's, thanks to Conte's services; after an inquiry from McCoy she began looking for deals, both inside and outside of the BMX world, that would recognize his value as a leading talent. In late 1987, Conte put an ambitious and potentially groundbreaking deal on the table, one that included McCoy's Haro teammate and riding partner Joe Johnson.

My manager had been looking into options for Joe and me, and she came back with a group of companies that would make up one deal. We were going to be riding for Adidas, who would provide clothing and shoes, and there was also a car dealership interested. Huffy was going to provide us both with frames, which would be custom-made by Kastan, and I would have a signature model. Then Jim Ford flew me out to California to look at a renewed deal with Haro…these guys were not only my employers, they were my friends. We discussed the situation and they made a very decent offer. But the advice we were getting was that the alternative deal would be better for us in the long run, so in late 1987 we signed contracts in Kansas City, and faxed them off. By the time we had arrived in Palmetto in January 1988 to compete in the AFA Masters, we fully believed we were riding under the new arrangement, but there was a problem. Micki was playing hardball with Huffy and had refused to sign the contract because it made her jointly liable for any breach of contract. We found out in Florida that the deal had collapsed and although Haro countered, they offered a lot less.

They had recently signed Mat [Hoffman] and with the industry heading down after a really dismal Christmas sales period, budgets were getting tight. There was never any animosity, in fact very little changed. I continued to ride a Haro Master and I often roomed with Bill Hawkins at contests. It was just a set of circumstances mixed with some bad timing.

– Dennis McCoy

would become the busiest and most diverse 12 months of freestyle-contest activity of the '80s era. The expansion and establishment of Haro pro Ron Wilkerson's 2Hip King of Vert half-pipe series continued to lead the sport into exciting new territory. In 1988, he delivered another new concept that reflected the evolved lifestyle of the riders with his 2Hip Meet the Street series. Street riding, the seed from which the freestyle concept had risen in the late 1970s, represented the simplest form of expression; to break new ground required nothing more than a bike and a fertile mind. The first Meet the Street was held in a vacant parking lot in Santee, near Lakeside in Southern California, on April 30, 1988. A day of pure innovation and experimentation crystalized the raw, energetic, and potentially anarchic image of the sport. In an instant, it seemed, the future direction of freestyle changed profoundly in the eyes of the watching world.

In ways that starkly contrasted the activities of the 2Hip movement, the AFA was also considering its next move. Founder and president Bob Morales, who had been drawn away from the day-to-day operations of the organization, began searching for a successor. A highly successful 1987 contest season, along with reports of staggering growth in the market, had created confidence within the industry. Consequently, the AFA embarked on

a formidable year of activity in 1988, starting with eight individual Masters events across the entire region of North America and culminating in a high-profile finals weekend at the 7-Eleven Velodrome in Carson City, California. But a disappointing attendance at the AFA Masters season opener in Palmetto, Florida became a sign of the times for the sport and the AFA. With Wilkerson's energetic 2Hip events grabbing headlines and diverting the vert scene into its own specialist direction and the ABA BMX racing organization diversifying with its own Freestyle Nationals contest series, the AFA now had genuine competition in the freestyle contest arena.

The departures of Dennis McCoy and Joe Johnson at the beginning of 1988 brought new faces to the Haro freestyle team. Sixteen-year-old prodigy Mat Hoffman had spent 18 months riding for rival brand Skyway, although an opportunity to move teams came in early 1988 via a deal brokered by Bob Haro's younger brother. Ron Haro, who had worked for Haro Designs since early 1981, had worked his way up from a support role on the first Haro freestyle Tour to becoming the manager of the newly formed Haro racing team in 1986. By all accounts, his rise was interesting as well as swift. After assuming responsibility for the smooth running of the warehouse in 1982, Ron had been ceremoniously demoted by Jim Ford following the arrival of Bill Hawkins, due to what he jokingly facetiously recalls as "maturity issues." But in 1984, a successful summer on the road with his brother, Ron Wilton, and Rich Sigur, plus having successfully convinced Jim Ford to let him work in the sales department, landed Ron back in Carlsbad. when a series of budget cuts were handed down in 1987 by Haro's parent company, Medalist, Ron made

Windy Osborn tracks Dennis McCoy at the 1987 Velodrome AFA
Finals. His last contest of the era in Haro colors.

Dave Nourie, the consummate entertainer. 1988 Haro Tour of Kings.

Two teams would occasionally meet up on tour, but we were all over the place and there was so much ground to cover. Touring was a great environment to develop new tricks. We were riding so much that you were able to progress new ideas. The Abubaca and Nothing were both developed on tour. Brian and Dave and I worked hard to improve the show format as much as we could. There was a science to performing and getting people into it.

– Ron Wilkerson

the ultimate sacrifice and offered to leave. His typical generosity was rewarded later in the year, however, when fate and a call from his older brother led him to the position of Skyway Freestyle Team Manager––and a strong, almost brotherly bond with star rider Hoffman. At the end of '87, when Ron returned to a more-prosperous Haro Designs in Carlsbad, he brought with him the option for Haro to sign young Mat, who was currently mulling over a disappointing contract renewal offer from Skyway.

Another new face, seemingly from out of nowhere, arrived in Carlsbad in November of 1986 when East Coast flatland specialist Joe Gruttola signed on at Haro Designs. Having entered the AFA Masters Series Finals at the Velodrome in Carson City with very little fuss or expectation, Joe had traveled from his parents' Long Island home with a plan to stay with a friend's family. A unanimous victory in the 14–15 Expert Flatland class forged a new destiny for the young talent, however. After a chance discussion with Haro associate John Peterson at a local riding spot the following day, Joe found himself at the Haro HQ discussing a sponsorship deal.

Meanwhile, in San Antonio, Texas, a talented young vert rider named Eben Krackau was emerging out of the local AFA contest ranks. Krackau had transitioned to freestyle in 1985, after a short but successful spell as a BMX racer. Haro's freestyle team manager Bill Hawkins quickly identified the young Texan as a prodigious talent, but it wasn't until practice for the 1987 Masters finals at the Velodrome in Carson City that Hawkins and Haro Vice President Jim Ford made their approach. In

January of 1988, Krackau announced his arrival on the Haro team in style by taking first place in vert at the first round of the AFA Masters in Palmetto, Florida.

A surprising new Team Haro recruit was an Englishman, Lee Reynolds, who had stepped onto US soil for the first time in March of 1988 as a member of the UK Hutch freestyle team. However, a disagreement with Hutch Team Manager Ron Stebenne over Reynolds's choice of after-show activities brought that arrangement to an abrupt conclusion. After a brief trip back to the UK to raise some capital, Reynolds returned to Leucadia and began riding for a Texas-based mail-order company called Trend. Within a year, he had connected with another UK freestyle export, former GT rider Jess Dyrenforth, and the two began riding local shows for Haro along with flatlander Ed Lenander.

With a new lineup in the riding ranks, and a record-breaking 120 individual show commitments, Team Haro rolled out of California in June of 1988 for the Tour of Kings. Touring was the highlight of the year for the riders. For those three months they were largely free of press commitments and the bureaucracy of the industry, with only one, very simple agenda: to energize the youth of the country by demonstrating the best of BMX freestyle. Ron Wilkerson, Brian Blyther, and Dave Nourie once again occupied one truck, while the relatively new team of Mat Hoffman, Joe Gruttola, and Rick Moliterno crewed the other.

As 1988 wound down, rumors of a decline on the sport's business end began to circulate. AFA contest attendances had also begun to tail

1988 2Hip King of Vert in Austin, Texas. Brian Blyther soars an "Invert" over the deck.

Ron Wilkerson during one of many contests and demos held at the Bercy Arena in Paris, France.

The 2Hip King of Vert comes to Paris France with "Bicross" magazine.

Lee was driving and he smelled smoke at around 5 a.m. Kevin and I were asleep in the back; we had just dropped Rick off at his house. We were woken up by smoke coming from the dashboard and by the time Lee was able to pull off the road, the smoke had turned into flames. Lee got out on the driver's side and ran. Kevin and I jumped out of the back door, climbed over the quarter-pipe in our underwear, and ran down the freeway before the whole thing exploded. By the time the police arrived, the truck was just twisted and burned metal, although the trailer was untouched. Those vans weren't built to pull such a heavy weight for so long and the transmission had caught fire. We were eventually supplied with a rental, but it had a limiter and we couldn't go over 55 mph. It became a very long journey at the end of a long tour.

– Jess Dyrenforth

The original Skate and BMX line up for the Swatch Impact Tour. Wilkerson would be replaced by Haro's Mat Hoffman following a mid air collision with Blyther in rehearsal.

off. With the cost of facilitating and insuring the series continuing to escalate, it was becoming more difficult to balance the books. Plus, the organization had recently relocated to Ohio and was under new leadership from promoter Randy Loop. But, even more important, the introduction of the 2Hip King of Vert Half-Pipe Series created a stark contrast between the AFA formula and the vision of the leading vert riders. The AFA's sustained faith in its tried-and-true quarter-pipe formula had created frustration within the vert ranks and, in the opinion of some, had hindered progress. But the AFA was taking giant steps forward in the flatland discipline. Although the intense rolling battles among Dennis McCoy, Haro's Rick Moliterno, and Martin Aparijo were captivating freestyle fans, the organization was beginning to resemble a specialist flatland arena; within a year, they would abandon vert completely.

In the late 1980s, it became increasingly clear that the habitual lifestyles and beliefs of the top riders were influencing and reinventing the image of the sport. In November of that year, a watershed moment indicative of the scene's chaotic evolution played out over the AFA Masters Finals weekend in Wichita. It involved Dennis McCoy, who had hit the form of his life in both the flatland and vert disciplines during the contest season and fought off stiff competition from not only Haro's Rick Moliterno but also numerous others in the vert ranks to walk away with the Vert, Flatland, and Overall titles. Furthermore, McCoy made his clean sweep in a year when he was without a bike-company sponsor—an achievement that directly reflected the industry's poor financial state and lack of confidence in its long-term future.

Haro's Ron Wilkerson put much of his energy throughout 1988 into his 2Hip organization, with the aim of delivering the sport's first genuine street contest. His weekend at the Wichita AFA Finals had a less-positive outcome, however,

after a life-threatening crash during his final vert run. On level points for the title, Ron had held back a new trick, the Nothing Air, which he had developed during the Haro summer tour. At Wichita, "nothing" lived up to its name when Ron took both hands and feet off the bike 8 feet above the deck and, in a sickening moment, hung up his front wheel on re-entry. The injuries he sustained put him into a coma for three days. The freestyle community immediately rallied, with Mat Hoffman's father converting his own light aircraft into an air ambulance to safely deliver Ron back to his home in Leucadia following his discharge from hospital. The incident would become a life-changing experience for Wilkerson. His recovery, which required him to learn to ride a bike again, resulted in a changed outlook and an even-more-relentless determination to push the sport into new territory.

The disappointing sales trend that had closed 1988 and opened 1989 proved to be more than just a bump in the road: sales of BMX bikes had precipitously declined over the year. With a team of high-profile riders commanding significant salaries and overheads, Jim Ford and Bob Haro found themselves in a tighter position than most. The only way out was cutbacks: team members received letters about these in January 1989; by the end of the year, long-serving teammates Ron Wilkerson, Dave Nourie, and Brian Blyther had decided to move on. A scaled-back summer Tour of Kings that year saw Haro dispatch star riders Rick Moliterno, Lee Reynolds, and Joe Gruttola, along with announcer Kevin Martin, deep into the Midwest and beyond. Just when it looked as if things couldn't get any worse, in a cruel twist of fate the Haro tour truck burst into flames during the 20-hour drive back to California at the conclusion of the tour. Nobody was injured, but the accident summed up the position of the company as well as the downturn of the BMX market.

Brian Blyther spins a 540 around skater Kevin Staab.

The year 1990 represented a dark period in the early history of BMX. Haro had seen its business peak at over $12 million at the conclusion of the 1987 fiscal year, only to see it decline by more than half within the turbulent 12 months of 1988. But Haro wasn't the only business that was suffering. At the end of the 1989 season, the AFA had finally concluded its national business in BMX and folded down its tents for the last time, after a difficult year of staging flatland events in low-key venues. The BMX press was also winded after a hard fight to reinvent and re-energize the scene. In a move dictated by the need to reduce costs, Wizard Publications decided to merge Freestylin' with its race-dedicated BMX Action magazine to create Go. With advertising revenue from within the industry all but gone, and page counts falling, the future of freestyle and its infrastructure was looking less and less assured by the week. But all was not lost.

As the industry fought for survival, a new movement was gathering pace. The late 1980s and early '90s would give rise to a number of rider-owned initiatives, born from a new-found freedom of choice that came with the ethos of, and belief in, having nothing left to lose. Belief in the future of the sport was alive and well among a group of core riders who would, as the '90s unfolded, direct it into a new era with subcultural brands and a hunger to take ownership of every aspect of the freestyle scene.

One of these riders, former racer and BMX Action test rider Chris Moeller, had often been left wanting by the quality and performance of the bikes he tested. His answer was to design and produce his own product ranges under his own brand, S&M. Ron Wilkerson's WAL (Wilkerson Air Lines), which emerged in late 1989, was also motivated by a need for better hardware during this period when the established brands were fighting for survival without the luxury of healthy research-and-development budgets.

The 1980s had seen the emergence, evolution, and demise of an exciting new youth sport. But as the old proverbs counsel, the night is darkest just before the dawn. And the sun will rise again.

The Orlando mall transitions, 1988. FREESTYLIN' photographer Spike Jonze door carves on a Coral Haro Master.

D.C. VERT
13

2 colm?

Phoenix, Arizona, January 1991. Mat Hoffman carves a huge air at the 2Hip Thrasher land contest.

1987 Washington DC, 2Hip King of Vert. Brian Blyther rises over Hoffman, Mike D and the UK's Skyway rider; Carlo Griggs.

Eben competes for Haro at the AFA finals, in November 1988 in Wichita, Kansas. Spike Jonze and John Kerr capture a "Candy Wrapper".

1985. Young Eben sits aboard his 1984 Haro Master at home in Texas.

16 | EBEN KRACKAU

The pivotal moment in 13-year-old Eben Krackau's freestyle career arrived in November of 1987. The young Texan was accustomed to being a long way from home as he and his father spent long weekends in pursuit of Eben's BMX ambitions. This particular journey had brought him to the 7-Eleven Velodrome in Carson City, a suburb of southern Los Angeles, where he was heavily favored in the finals of the AFA's National Masters Freestyle Series. And sure enough, after his victory in the 13 and Under Expert Ramp Division, the weekend concluded on an even more positive note. As he practiced in preparation for the contest, Eben had been blissfully unaware of two individuals observing him from behind the ramp: Bill Hawkins, Haro's Freestyle Team Manager and Jim Ford, the company's vice president. The conversation that took place moments later, as Eben removed his gloves and full-face helmet, changed the course of his young life.

Like many other freestyler riders of the era, Eben's story in BMX began at his local BMX track in San Antonio. His father, a motocross fanatic who counted AMA National Motocross Champion Kent Howerton among his friends, had introduced his son to the sport at an early age. Although he desperately wanted to race in the thriving local MX scene, a chronic medical condition made it too dangerous. Instead, Eben was faced with to the task of finding an alternative way to compete on two wheels.

By 1986, Eben was immersed in BMX and hanging out with a group of locals who dreamed of rising from the backyard scene into the national spotlight. The launch in early 1986 of the AFA's newest concept, The National Masters Freestyle series had helped the organization begin to develop a network of local promoters around the country to collaborate on staging smaller amateur contests that would help develop the sport at the grassroots level. In early February, promoter and local GT Race Team Manager Scott Patterson brought the AFA to the Austin City Coliseum for the first affiliated event in Texas. The contest, held over a weekend, aimed to provide a genuine opportunity for locals to compete in a nationally regulated and recognized event. This particular arrangement would also bring to Austin two members of the GT factory freestyle team, Eddie Fiola and Martin Aparijo; there, the international stars would carry out a freestyle demonstration in the break between the flatland and ramp classes.

The demo was held under some strange light-show setup. When Eddie or Martin rode, each of them had an individual spotlight tracking them while the rest of the building was completely dark. Now I can only imagine the nightmare that it was to ride the quarter-pipe under those conditions, but I was a kooky little kid then and thought it was cool. Walking into the coliseum was pretty surreal; there were tons of local freestyle riders, lots of bad haircuts…neon bikes and clothing everywhere. It was the first real freestyle event that I had been to besides Haro demos at Cuny's in San Antonio, and it was this event that convinced me to start competing.

– Eben Krackau

I was born with a brain tumor and when I was 3 years old it had to be surgically removed. This left me with a plastic plug in my head, and there was no way my mom was going to let me race motorcycles! I remember seeing coverage of Mike Buff and RL [Osborne] riding in a freestyle demo during the intermission of a motocross race at the Houston Astrodome. Kent [Howerton] and a local bike-shop owner named Glen Mulestein suggested BMX as a safer alternative to MX, and soon after that I was fitted for a Diamond Back mini at the shop. I started racing and did pretty well, but by 1984 I was pretty burned out on it and was having more fun just jumping and carving around in my neighborhood. That July I went to see Bob [Haro], Rich [Sigur], and Ron [Wilton] perform a freestyle show at Cuny's Bike shop in San Antonio, and that was it. Within a year I had a 6 x 8 quarter-pipe in the back yard…and it was on.

– Eben Krackau

The pivotal moment. 1987 AFA Masters final, Velodrome. Eben "Fakies" his way to deal on the Haro Freestyle team.

The Velodrome in late '86 was my first opportunity to compete against riders from outside the state. I rode pretty well and by this time I had added Foot-Plants, Fly-Outs and Roll-Ins to my trick list. I took second place behind Robbie Van Patten [Ted Emmer's protégé] who was going 7 feet out and riding to Metallica. It was definitely an eye-opener for me. Robbie made me realize that I could go a lot higher and motivated me to want to beat him the next time we competed against each other. I was on quite a steep learning curve after that.

– Eben Krackau

As the 1987 AFA season began, a more versatile, refined, and confident Eben Krackau emerged from his short winter break. The long, intense backyard vert sessions were about to pay off in a series of impressive performances in which he would dominate his division at local level. In May, in Austin, he encountered a young rider who would become a good friend as well as his toughest competitor throughout the later decade. Ryan Dunman had risen out of the busy local freestyle scene in Camarillo, Southern California, to secure a sponsorship deal with Dyno, a freestyle bike and accessories brand founded in 1984 by the AFA's Bob Morales. Through the next 18 months, the division's two best riders would regularly duke it out in a series of AFA contests that often ended in a tie, to be decided by run-off. For Eben, June of 1987 included a landmark return to Los Angeles and a victory in the Converse Pro Freestyle Contest—his first national contest win outside of his home state. After a frustrating second place at the AFA Masters Series Round 5 in October, in Wayne, New Jersey, in November the freestyle world would gather in Compton, a Los Angeles neighbourhood, for the AFA Series Finals at the Dominguez Hills Velodrome––and the moment the 13-year-old Texan had been dreaming about.

The Austin contest was locally rated as a huge success, and within a few weeks a series of smaller events held in schoolyards, at bike shops, and at BMX races began to connect riders from across the state. This spate of organic growth created a serious uplift in demand for more regular events, and in mid-May, the AFA returned to central Texas to host an even more ambitious occasion—this time at the Fiesta Plaza Mall, east of downtown San Antonio. For 12-year-old Eben Krackau, the weekend was a giant step in an exciting direction. Tasting victory for the first time at a recognized contest, he formed up with a group of locals and embarked on a period of development that would revolve around long weekends and evenings riding and testing his limits on the backyard half-pipe. Six months later, in November, appearances by Haro's Dennis McCoy and Ron Wilkerson at a regional AFA contest once again showed the local amateur scene what it would take to reach the national ranks. It was that November that Eben and his mom headed to Los Angeles from their home in San Antonio for the finals of th eAFA Masters, an opportunity for the young Texan to compete with and observe the best national freestyle riders in the country.

I rode the pipeline the day before the comp, and felt mentally ready. The day of the event, it was super-damp outside, which limited the number of ramps we were able to practice on. Before my run, unbeknownst to me, Bill Hawkins and Jim Ford were standing behind the wedge ramp watching me practice. I believe I rode first in the contest, and did every variation I had. I rode off the riding area and started to take my helmet and pads off, and when I looked up, Bill and Jim were standing in front of me. I had no idea who either of them was but Bill told me that I rode really well and asked me if I wanted to join the Haro team. He gave me a Haro Air Wear decal with his name and phone number scribbled on the back and said to call him the following week.

– Eben Krackau

The sponsorship arrangement with Haro would set the young Texan up for the toughest and most productive year of his new career. With a full season of national AFA Masters contests slated into a busy calendar that also included the 2Hip King of Vert series and shorter tours during the summer, the frenetic BMX freestyle world seemed to be constantly on the move. A positive start to the year saw Eben take back-to-back victories in the AFA season openers in Palmetto, Florida, and Portland, Oregon. A run out at a local AFA contest in Fort Worth, Texas, along with a well-earned break during the Arizona AFA contest, set Eben up for a big summer of intense competition. In the meantime, he had turned 14, and his strength, skill, and technical ability on a bike were all in steep upward curves. Now pushing around 8 feet above coping on a regular basis, his runs––teeming with technical variations like Top-Side No-Footed Can-Cans, Candy Bars, and huge Lookdown Fakies–– would set the bar high within the division. A return to action at the AFA Masters in Austin brought Eben another first place, despite a concussion sustained the day before while street riding with teammate Mat Hoffman.

The Summer of big air. 1988 at Jay Hakala's house.

I personally feel that the '88 Texas AFA Masters comp in Austin was the beginning of the shift in BMX. Freestyle seemed so huge at the time and it felt as if it was going to continue to grow. The Haro team took it into their own hands to do something different at this comp: most of the team rode in Haro t-shirts or Haro demo tops, shorts, and Haro tech kneepads. I remember Wilkerson's run really well. It consisted of about 95 percent lip tricks, which at the time was completely unheard of. Most pros went for big air, and lip tricks didn't ever seem to get judged on how technically difficult they actually were.

– Eben Krackau

The first six months of the Haro deal passed in a blur of almost constant riding, traveling, competition, and keeping up with schoolwork. Contests would bring the team together from the four corners of the country, and intensely focused weekends of riding and fighting for points would often see the team prevail in a range of different categories and age groups. Then, when the lights went down in the early evening, riders and friends from opposing teams would often form up and set out on local expeditions to explore new riding spots.

1988 was such an amazing year and ended up on a relatively high note. I ended my year as the AFA Masters 14 Expert Ramp Champion, the Texas AFA 14¬–15 Expert Ramp Champion, and Texas AFA Freestyler of the Year. After the Masters Finals in Wichita, Spike [Jonze] told me to stop by Mat [Hoffman]'s house on the way home to shoot some photos for Freestylin', which was at the time a dream come true and an unexpected way to end the year. Not only was I getting to go to Mat's house and warehouse to ride with him, I was also getting to shoot photos with Spike. I honestly couldn't believe it. It was truly an amazing day.

– Eben Krackau

September 1988, Gonzales, Texas AFA freestyle demo. Huge "Nose Bone Air" on a sweet transition.

The 1989 2Hip King of Vert in Colorado Springs. A "One Footed Invert" on a prototype 1989 Haro Master.

In September of 1988, the AFA Masters series rolled into the vast Midwestern city of Columbus, Ohio. As usual, the contest would provide some memorable moments. Haro's East Coast vert specialist, Jeremy Alder, would register a rare breakthrough moment for the now highly evolved sport by pulling the first 360 Bar Spin ever seen in a contest. Haro's Rick Moliterno would walk away with the weekend's AFA Overall Pro title, and the contest would welcome the first appearance of the French BLIX Haro team of David Chabert and Jean Somsois. For Eben Krackau it was business as usual, as he once again found the form he needed to take the weekend's top honors in his division. But as the November AFA Masters Series Finals weekend loomed into view, the foundations of the sport were beginning to

look less assured. News of the disintegration of the Skyway Recreation Factory Team on the eve of the Columbus contest had left many in shock. At the series' hastily arranged Round 7, in Los Angeles, the Compton Velodrome had been almost empty of spectators. And with the lowest attendance of the year occurring at the series finals in Wichita, Kansas, this series would become the last multidiscipline AFA event of the era.

The year 1989 would bring different challenges for the professional freestyle community. Unsettling rumors relating to the future of the AFA organization directed the focus of the hardcore riders almost entirely toward the 2Hip King of Vert and Meet the Street contests. Having competed at the infamous 2Hip King of Vert Texas Barge Jam in July of 1988, Eben understood what was expected, and began to focus on developing a series of new tricks. At the time, the 2Hip format represented the epitome of the progressive modern vert scene. A half-pipe format, with few if any enforced rules, was meant to encourage creativity, experimentation, and a community feel among the competitors. But the stakes were high and, accordingly, the quality of riding was undoubtedly the best and most progressive of the era.

I started preparing for the 1989 contest season with a goal in mind…if the AFA was going to continue with its quarter-pipe contests, then I would aim to turn pro at the last comp of the year. Haro had planned for me to come out to Carlsbad to do shows during spring break and sign my new contract for '89. But two weeks before the California trip, I was practicing 540s and late in the day I landed a little sideways and slammed. I ended up going down pretty hard and breaking my clavicle in four places. This took me out for around six weeks. When I ended up going out to Cali a couple

of months later, I arrived at Haro on a Monday morning, and the first person I saw was Bob—which, incidentally, was the coolest thing since I had never really met him before. He gave me a set of sample gloves and showed me the new bash guard, Haro Master, which was in development. The contract negotiation was a little daunting, and even as a 15-year-old kid I was still aware that the sport was heading into a period of collapse. The offer was beyond my wildest dreams, but I had already decided that in such uncertain times for BMX, I needed to keep my options open.

– Eben Krackau

Eben would continue to represent Haro Designs at contest level throughout the summer of 1990, before joining RL Osborn's Bully brand, Ron Wilkerson WAL, more recentlt Austin - based Homeless Bikes.As the freestyle scene ebbed and flowed through the early 1990's, Eben would become one of a group of riders who would keep the faith, and continue to ride and energize a scene that existed largely away from the media spotlight.

I was a young kid riding a BMX bike getting paid and having a blast, traveling to contests, and hanging out with the riders who a year earlier I had been watching in a demo at my local bike shop. Riding for Haro was definitely a plus. I had the best bikes and traveled with the best riders, and they were all guys who I pretty much idolized. We had a great team manager in Bill, who supported us and made us feel like a family. Dave Nourie was the first person I met when I joined Haro, and he made sure I didn't feel left out. He introduced me to everyone I hadn't met. If my dad wasn't able to travel to a contest, it was Moliterno who made sure my bike was dialed in. It was like I immediately had six or seven older brothers who were some of the best freestyle BMX riders in the world.

– Eben Krackau

I remember being in my back yard learning to do wheelies. I obviously didn't really know BMX as a sport or an industry at that point; I was just riding in my back yard figuring it out every day. Having fun in the process.

– Mat Hoffman

Thrasherland 2Hip Finals in Phoenix, Arizona, January 1991.
Hoffman spins a huge 900.

April 1991.The 2Hip Lemon Grove ramp demo. Hoffman broke forks regularly and is using forks from a 1984 Haro Master.

My uncle was a carpenter. We took some plans that were published in BMX Action magazine and built this little 6-foot quarter-pipe in the yard. I remember being on top of that ramp looking down while we were trying to figure out who was going to be the first person to drop in. My brother held me there, right on the lip, and said, 'I'm just going to let you see what it looks like.' I was terrified, but I trusted him, and he dropped me and I rolled out. From that moment, I was like 'OK, what else can I do?' It was that feeling that gave me the freedom and confidence to keep creating moments like that.

– Mat Hoffman

17 | MAT HOFFMAN

The year 1988 saw the arrival at Haro Designs of a 16-year-old vert rider from rural Oklahoma named Mathew Hoffman. His journey to the gates of the thriving international freestyle scene is a tale of a teenager's obsession with the dynamics of a sport that would inspire and ultimately define him as a young man. In the summer of 1986, when he entered and won the 14/15 and Under Expert Vert Division at the high-profile AFA Masters Series held at Madison Square Garden in New York City, the freestyle world changed in an instant. Having arrived at MSG with his immediate family, his chest protector, a full-face helmet, and a gut full of nervous energy in anticipation of his national contest debut, Hoffman would leave Manhattan having achieved everything he had dreamed about as a kid with a bike. His story in BMX ––a testament to his remarkable contribution to the sport––has already been told, but his years of riding alongside his heroes on the all-star Haro Freestyle Team in the late 1980s is an example of relentless innovation and one modest teenager's determination to energize and reinvent the parameters of vert riding.

Hoffman's daily routine as a kid growing up in Oklahoma revolved around a simple but intense connection to the sport that would ultimately define him as a pioneer in the action sports community. Like many other top riders from the era, the liberation of simply riding and creating while floating high above the deck had an almost hypnotic effect. The rural lifestyle of Oklahoma, and a family life that revolved around close relationships with his brothers, sister, and parents, kept him apart from the media buzz and business politics of the sport and left him both focused and blissfully undistracted. When the opportunity to ride in front of a small gathering presented itself, at the local Mountain Dew bottling plant, a moment of chance speculation on the part of his mom created a swell of anticipation in the BMX press.

The breakthrough at MSG resulted in opportunities and decisions for Hoffman that were both numerous and immediate. Moments after his final vert run at the contest, he was under siege from the Skyway and Haro freestyle team managers with offers of sponsorships and tours.

Skyway's Eddie Roman and Maurice Meyer were able to begin successful contract negotiations with Hoffman's mom The arrangement they eventually settled on would bring Mat together with Skyway's team manager, Ron Haro, for the first time. Ron, known as Rhino to his friends, had recently departed his older brother's company in the wake of budget cuts; in fact, he had volunteered to leave in light of a belief that with his surname, he could secure another job in BMX more easily than others at the company. The two quickly became close friends; later, the charismatic Rhino would figure prominently in Hoffman's career. Now, it would be Ron who helped to create the next opportunity for the rising star.

In early '87, Bob called Ken Costner at Skyway to recommend me for a job, and soon after that I moved to Redding in Northern California to become Skyway's Freestyle Team Manager. In late '87, Jim Ford called me and invited me to come back and work with Bill [Hawkins], selling tours and announcing at shows. They knew that Mat and I had become close; he was like a little brother to me. In the wake of some slow months, and with Mat's reputation as a rider continuing to grow, Skyway made an offer to renew Mat's contract that was pretty disappointing. Haro had just lost Dennis [McCoy], and after we talked it was clear that Mat was pretty excited to ride for Haro. Over the New Year's holiday I met with Jim and we worked something out. I felt bad that we walked out on Skyway, especially because of Ken Costner, but it was ultimately a business decision in a period where the sport was becoming huge. Plus we were homesick, and I really missed working at Haro.

– Ron Haro

The deal that brought Mat Hoffman to Haro Designs was signed and sealed in January of 1988. His first contest outing in Haro colors came in February, at the ABA National Freestyle contest at the Velodrome in Carson City, although the occupational hazard of a broken leg (while learning 540s on his warehouse ramp in Oklahoma) kept him out of action for the season openers, including the first round of the 2Hip King of Vert in early March. Mat reappeared in April, at the AFA Masters in Tucson, 90 percent recovered and wearing a knee brace that clearly didn't hinder his progress as he continued to dominate with an impressive run full of multiple height variations. An opportunity to join the 2Hip crew for an invitational jam at the Paris Bercy Arena arrived in March. A group of the best freestyle riders in the US, along with a group of high-profile skaters including Tony Hawk, Christian Hosoi, Danny Way, and Kevin Staab, traveled to the French capital to ride in the 2Hip King of Vert Invitational (the skaters formed part of the larger Mega Free Combined Event). The move to Haro had been an exciting prospect for Hoffman, but the summer ahead would become one of the busiest in his early career.

Haro was always like the dream team. Ron got talking with his bro; he was thinking about leaving Skyway at the time. I was close to Ron, we really bonded, and I said, 'Dude, I want to follow you.' I was riding a lot and getting some magazine covers and it felt like good timing for me. I wasn't really aware of what hype was, but the opportunity to ride for Haro, on the same team as Wilkerson and Blyther, was amazing.

– Mat Hoffman

The Haro Tour of Kings rolled out of Carlsbad in early June of 1988. This particular tour would not only crystalize the pinnacle of global BMX popularity, it would also be the last time that Haro

dispatched two individual teams in the U.S. in one summer. Fresh from a trip to Europe, the tried-and-tested partnership of Ron Wilkerson, Brian Blyther, and Dave Nourie headed north, taking in local California spots before heading to Oregon and beyond. A separate team of relatively new recruits consisting of pro all-rounder Rick Moliterno, expert flatlander Joe Gruttola, and vert specialist Hoffman, would travel straight to the East. Ron Haro joined the trio as the tour announcer. As usual, there would be plenty to talk about at the end of the summer.

On top of this busy year of touring, the late 1980s was brimming with opportunities to compete. The expansion of the 2Hip King of Vert series would prove to be a perfect environment for Hoffman, who could pump a half-pipe better than most and whose huge repertoire of multiple trick variations often set the standard across all divisions. The series was considered among the riders to be the most progressive environment for trick development; not surprisingly, it produced some of the most innovative moments of the decade. The camaraderie and loose atmosphere at the contests settled Hoffman into a rich vein of form. In the Expert category, which included stiff competition from accomplished riders including Dino Deluca, Dave Voelker, Chris Potts, and Lee Reynolds, Mat would compete and dominate the amateur division for the remainder of the decade.

In January of 1989, after the 2Hip King of Vert finals in Irvine, Southern California, 17-year-old Mat Hoffman stepped up and turned pro. But the arrangement with Haro had begun to falter. In March, to the surprise of his fellow competitors, in March Hoffman arrived at the King of Vert first round in Toronto as a free agent.

My parents were extremely supportive and they helped me to fund and build a 9-foot-tall portable quarter-pipe. We took it down to the parking lot of the local Mountain Dew bottling plant and set it up to see if we could get them to sponsor us as a team. Somebody took a photograph of me and sent it to my mom. I wasn't aware at the time that she had sent it into the guys at Freestylin' magazine, but she did and Lew published it. That's when things really started to take off.

– Mat Hoffman

January 1990. The 1989 2Hip King of Vert finals were held in Newport Beach. Hoffman "Body Jar's" on a prototype frame that would become the 1990 Haro Sport.

Despite his departure from Haro, Hoffman's weekend in Toronto would be remembered for another remarkable moment. During one of his final runs, he successfully spun the first 900 in a contest. The trick had become the preoccupation of a number of senior riders, although the timing and power required to rotate and successfully land a 900 had so far eluded the sport's top riders. Hoffman's breakthrough moment came within days of his departure from Haro. Within a year, however, he would be back in California wearing Haro colors.

The new contract signaled the start of a two-year period of devastating form that would ultimately redefine the parameters of the sport, both in the eyes of the fan base and in the view of the riders. The 900 in Toronto became the first of three breakthrough tricks developed and delivered by Hoffman within a dynamic two-year period of experimentation. In 1989, he arrived at the second Mega Free in Paris still reeling from a huge slam the day before, on his own ramp back in Oklahoma. After tense 24-hour period during which he could barely remember who he was, Hoffman was able to drop in and enjoy an eventful weekend both on and off the ramp. The group that weekend included the elite of the US skate and freestyle scenes as well as journalists and photographers, one of whom was future music video and Hollywood film director Spike Jonze.

The next period truly defined Hoffman's ability, as well as his character and commitment to the sport. In March of 1990, in a moment of unflinching genius, he dispatched the Flip Fakie, an acrobatic feat that even the best-informed riders had never considered to be possible.

Early Days. Hoffman on the "Enchanted Ramp" in Leucadia, CA, in April 1988.

You lived in a van pretty much for three months. For a little kid riding on the greatest team of the era was like a dream. Rhino was a crazy dude, although he knew exactly when to be responsible and he really looked after us well. Joe was a New Yorker and he had a different flavor—very progressive, into making music and with his own unique style. Rick could do everything really well. He was a pretty intense personality and it wasn't difficult to get on his bad side, but after a while we all settled down. We had to work out quickly how to balance the show. We were three different riders, all different ages, and we all brought something unique to the team. There was sometimes tension. To begin with I would just start blasting the vert ramp straight away, and I learned that for the show to work we had to build it up into something. We all had to continually think about that balance.

– Mat Hoffman

Changing times. The 2Hip "Meet the Street" contest in La Jolla, CA. Hoffman "Indian Air's" over the jump box.

I used to drop in with a list of tricks taped to my frame, but when I was on the Swatch Impact Tour in '88, I met a skater named Jeff Philips. When you ride and compete with the same guys a lot you get to know people's best tricks and the order of their run, and you can pretty much call the tricks in order. Watching Jeff, I noticed that every time he dropped in he did something different, and it would always be awesome. I said, 'Hey Jeff, How do you come up with your run?' He said, 'I don't, I just let each wall tell me what's going to happen on the next wall.' It made a lot of sense, so I started doing the same thing. I was always happy with my run after that and I live my life like that now.

– Mat Hoffman

Times were getting tough in BMX due to a big drop-off in business. Mat and I left Haro and moved to Oklahoma to start up a new venture with his dad, named VIP Concepts. We wanted to start staging our own shows. Mat Sr. was running the company and had funded the building of a portable half-pipe. We were talking to a couple of interested corporations and flew to California to talk to a bike brand about sponsorship. We showed them pictures of the ramp and when we left, they went into their workshop and built two of them! Mat Sr. was keen to start a bike brand, but it felt too risky at the time and we returned to California where Mat Jr. re-signed with Haro. Leaving Oklahoma was a big regret of mine for years as the Hoffmans were like family to me.

– Ron Haro

The Texas "Barge Jam" held in Austin was a challenge for the riders. Hoffman "Bar Hops" on a Haro Sport.

I started doing a lot of street stuff. I was trying to figure out how we could slide on the bottom bracket and after some discussions with the guys at Haro; I helped to bring the Bashguard idea to reality on the Master. I also helped with the evolution of a number of ideas at that time because it seemed like things were changing and that the energy for reinvention at the bike companies wasn't there. I suggested that they make plastic pegs that worked better on rails, and stuff like that. But then ideas would come back from the factory and they wouldn't be made from the right materials. So I was knocking myself out a lot and breaking forks regularly. I was trying to push the sport forward and the technology of the bikes couldn't really keep up.

– Mat Hoffman

Later that year, at the UK King of Vert in Mansfield, England, he confirmed that he had learned to rotate and refine the trick when he unleashed the Flair, another near-incomprehensible feat of aerial mastery in which he not only landed the trick ,but also successfully rolled out facing the next wall. Nor was Hoffman's innovation confined to the vert ramp. Through the early 1990s he played a significant role in the development of street riding, demonstrating the same total disregard for his personal safety and bringing some of his evolved vert skills to Wilkerson's 2Hip King of Dirt and Meet the Street series. In addition to his role as a leading and innovative rider, he demonstrated insightful qualities while contributing to the design of the first Bashguard frame, the 1989 Haro Master, in collaboration with Haro's president and lead designer, Bob Haro.

The year 1991 would signal the end of Mat Hoffman's three-year association with the Haro brand. In the wake of a decline in the sales of BMX bikes, and a perception within the riding ranks that the brands were starting to neglect the safety aspects of the sport, Hoffman became both frustrated and genuinely concerned about the quality of hardware that was trickling into the perishing freestyle market. There was no doubt that the brands were hurting from the steep decline in interest at the end of the 1980s; many had already begun to direct their resources toward their survival efforts within other cycling categories. Whether his frustration emerged from the perceived lack of interest on the part of the brands, or simply from the accelerated progress that Hoffman himself had driven beyond all expectations with a series of game-changing tricks, remains a point of conjecture.

The Austin Texas "Barge Jam", July,1988. Hoffman was one of very few riders able to master Ron Wilkerson's ambitous floating ramp . Here FREESTYLIN' photographer Spike Jonze captures a"Pervert Decade drop in"

Without question, Mathew Hoffman's contributions to the sport of freestyle BMX through the late 1980s and beyond are among the most profound and important of the sport's 35-year history. Within a year of his departure from Haro, Hoffman would address his industry-related concerns with a typical hands-on approach by creating his own BMX freestyle brand: Hoffman Bikes. Then, when the freestyle scene entered its darkest period and the corporations and marketers had become a distant memory, Hoffman battened down the hatches to help lead the sport into an era of reinvention. A period of performing freestyle shows at state fairs and shopping malls, with a group of trusted and committed friends, gave rise to a series of innovative, rider-organized events that would truly begin to wrestle the future direction of the sport back into the hands of the core. The corporations would return in the mid-1990s, looking for opportunities to capitalize on the evolved lifestyle aspects of freestyle, but the riders would now represent a more informed and unified group that would no longer stand back and be dictated to.

Haro's arrival on the National BMX racing scene, as a genuie Factory Team raised more than a few eyebrows, and came with a statment of intent. The RS1 Group 1 Race Bike.

There was a period when Lee and I were riding shows five days every week. Lee would leave Carlsbad in the Haro van and pick me up at my place. We did a lot of shows around Upland, close to the skate park. We would get a hotel for three or four nights and just ride school shows every day, sometimes two per day. I do remember it slowing down quite a bit and there were phone calls from Bill [Hawkins] and Ron [Haro] to keep us up to date. They were great guys and were pretty bummed when it ended.

– Jess Dyrenforth

Paris 2HIP Invitational, March 1989. Reynolds Tweaks a huge "Table" air on one of Rick Moliterno's longer custom Haro Master Frames.

18 | LEE REYNOLDS

During the late 1980s, Lee Reynolds became one of a handful of young British riders who relocated to the epicenter of the international freestyle world: Southern California. The UK scene had evolved similarly to the one in the US, but towards the end of the decade, the image and blueprint of the sport faltered at the hands of the disconnected UK governing body. Consequently, a number of talented young riders looked beyond the shores of Europe for their next opportunity. Lee Reynolds was one of them, and his journey across the Atlantic would land him a position on the greatest BMX freestyle team of the decade.

Lee was born in the English university town of Oxford, in 1970; when he was 5 years old, his family relocated to the Welsh town of Monmouth. He received a Diamond Back BMX for his tenth birthday and began racing at the Ross-on-Wye track a few miles north of town. As freestyle began to work its way into the UK BMX scene, local tracks would often stage contests over race weekends; Lee would enter and win his first in the parking lot of the Ross-on-Wye track before deciding to focus on freestyle full time. In 1985 the family relocated once again, this time to the town of Stony Stratford (about an hour north of London). As he became more independent, Lee began to connect with other committed riders; before long, he found himself competing in the UKBFA national freestyle series.

As the UK movement gathered momentum, the best riders would regularly form up for organized jams and contests to a series of key destinations. Backyard half-pipes and bike friendly skate parks in areas including Chingford, Banbury, Romford, Southsea, Harrow, and Livingston in Scotland brought the riders and BMX press together.

Inevitably, by the second half of the decade, a genuine freestyle community had formed. After entering a contest at the infamous Mons Ramp in 1986, Reynolds secured the first magazine shot of his freestyle career. The following year, he not only placed second in the 16 Expert Division of the Tizer BMX World Freestyle Championship, held in the UK, but did so while riding for Hutch Hi Performance, a leading international freestyle brand. But it was in March of 1988, in Paris, that Lee Reynolds' destiny would truly begin to take shape.

Throughout the latter 1980s, the Palais Omnisport Arena, located on Bercy Boulevard on the Right Bank of the River Seine in Paris, became a pivotal junction of the international freestyle scene. As the new sport flooded into Europe from the United States, the proactive and highly motivated owners of Bicross, the French BMX freestyle magazine, staged a series of ambitious race and freestyle events at the venue known simply as The Bercy.

I was on Hutch back in the UK, and in March of '88 I went to the Bercy 2HIP King of Vert contest in Paris as a spectator. That's where I first met some of the US riders ,including Chris Potts, who was also riding for Hutch in the States. A few weeks later I was on my way to California after Ron Stebenne (the Hutch guy in the US) connected me with 2Hip announcer Kevin Martin. I spent about a month at the Enchanted House on vacation. I did a photo shoot with Spike Jonze for Freestylin' and those shots gained me instant recognition in the US. It cost me my front teeth though. Spike found one of them 20 feet from where I slammed a big turndown. After that I went back to England, sold my car and everything else, and came back.

–Lee Reynolds

San Diego, 1988.

There was a good crew in Stony Stratford made up of BMX riders and skaters. We built a decent half-pipe at the local recreation ground called 'The Boat' which was really supportive of the local BMX and skate scene. I started entering UKBFA contests and the scene in London was probably the most progressive in the country at the time, so I was traveling down and getting to know some of the amazing young British riders who were pushing the scene forward. This is when I first met Nick Elkan, who introduced me to most of the local riders. Texan Greg Guillotte was in the UK, as was Hawaiian Andy Shohara. I was lucky that there were some really talented guys around like Mike Canning, Andy Brown, Jason Hassel, John Povah, Phil Dolan, Jason Ellis, and Frasier Campbell, to name a few.

–Lee Reynolds

Reynolds hangs out with vert rider John Byers during a photo-shoot with Brad McDonald.

On his return to California, Reynolds quickly settled into life at Enchanted house and prepared to begin representing Hutch in the 2Hip King of Vert Series. In May of 1988, he made his US debut at Round 2 in Flint, Michigan, where he placed an impressive third in the Expert Division (behind Haro's Mat Hoffman and GT's Dino Deluca). That contest weekend became Reynolds's first encounter with the high-profile riders of the US freestyle scene; as usual, the contest after-party would present alternative opportunities to test the known limits.

I got fired from the Hutch team due to an incident at the Flint 2Hip Contest. Basically they didn't agree with my late-night partying. It was when I first got to meet everybody I had seen in the magazines and I wanted to hang out. [Hutch team manager] Ron Stebenne had told me to go to bed earlier in the evening and didn't appreciate that I got back to the hotel at 8 a.m.

– Lee Reynolds

Departing Hutch created an unforeseen challenge for the young Englishman. At first, Ron Stebenne had proposed only suspending Reynolds for his after-hours antics, but after some discussion Lee decided to quit the team immediately. Returning bikeless from the weekend, he was now unable to ride. The problem turned out to be only a temporary inconvenience, however, thanks to Haro's Mat Hoffman. After a week of filming and photo shoots in Leucadia, Hoffman gifted Lee with his own Haro Sport. Then, within a month, a new opportunity surfaced for Reynolds. Housemate and landlord Kevin Martin was running a West Coast distribution office out of the Enchanted house's garage for Trend Bike Source, an Austin-based BMX mail-order company. An introduction to Trend's owner, Greg Hansen, at the 2Hip event in Flint in May, had developed into a friendship, and an arrangement followed for Reynolds to represent the brand at a national AFA contest.

The next 12 months showered bittersweet fortune on Lee Reynolds. A season of excellent placings at 2Hip and AFA contests throughout the 1988 season brought positive attention to his vert skills, but the business end of the sport was going into free-fall. As the scene and lifestyle of the core riders became more experimental, the image of the sport was becoming far less controlled. Before long, street riding had risen to the top of the agenda; accordingly, a series of landmark street-riding contests held in and around San Diego, facilitated by Ron Wilkerson's 2Hip Society, began to lead the sport in an alternative direction.

Airwalk Shoes Photo shoot on the "Enchanted Ramp", In Leucadia, CA.

Huge Stretched out "Can-Can-Look-back" in Leucadiia

Vert was my thing, so I didn't really go in for the street contests. It was Trend Bike Source that really helped me out when I parted ways with Hutch. They gave me a Haro Sport, all the parts I needed, and they paid for me to go to the Wichita AFA contest and compete. But that was the beginning of a bad period for all of us. Ron [Wilkerson] slammed hard at the contest and went into a coma. There were obviously a lot of worried people in the scene and at the ramp house back in leucadia. Ron came back though, and had a different outlook on life when he recovered.

But I always loved both Rons.

– Lee Reynolds

freestyle at grass-roots level. This project began when eccentric ex-GT rider Brian Scura approached Bill Hawkins, Haro's tour manager, to discuss a unique concept that he had developed and delivered for rival brand GT. The formula revolved around a trio of riders who would perform freestyle shows on a quarter-pipe at local schools, in an attempt to inspire and introduce a new generation of kids to freestyle. The riders considered the concept to be a little goofy, because it involved a strictly choreographed show and a presentation on bike safety, although they understood that the displays would ultimately serve to connect new audiences to the sport. Reynolds replaced German rider Berndt Schmidt, who had to return to Germany to complete his national service. He would join friend and fellow Englishman Jess Dyrenforth, who had

become a member of Scura's team for GT and also had become part of a deal in late 1988 that saw Scura sell his database of more than 100 shows to Haro.

As the school program wound down, the two riders would head in opposite directions. Within a few weeks Dyrenforth returned to the well-resourced GT team, which was embarking on a period of focused promotion meant to bring the ailing market back to prosperity.

As Reynolds continued to network with his connections in the San Diego area, his unique and natural skills on vert soon became his ticket to the opportunity that would establish him as a senior member of the Haro Freestyle Team. In February 1989, following a second trip to Paris

for the high profile Mega Free-hosted 2Hip King of Vert Invitational Jam, Reynolds's huge tweaked airs and multiple variations secured him a spot on that summer's Haro Tour of Kings.

One of the first times I remember meeting Bob [Haro] was in the warehouse at Haro when I was visiting Bill Hawkins. Bob handed me a prototype Haro Master frame with a Bashguard and a few weeks later I went out on the 1989 Haro summer tour with Rick [Moliterno], Joe [Gruttola], and Kevin [Martin]. It was my first real tour in the US, but with the downturn in freestyle interest it was a very different experience for Joe and Rick, who had both toured at the peak of the sport's popularity. At times, they were at war. Joe decided to leave partway through and was replaced by Jess. The Haro truck was on its last legs towards the end of that tour. My first time driving in New York, we were coming out of the Lincoln tunnel and the trailer hitch sheared off. We managed to drag it to a side street where this guy welded it back together. Then the truck caught fire on the way home when I was driving. It was a long eventful tour but a great experience.

– Lee Reynolds

On June 22n, the 1989 Haro Tour of Kings rolled out of Colorado Springs on what would be remembered as a highly eventful summer campaign. Unexpected, eventful encounters with the GT and Dyno factory freestyle teams throughout the summer gave rise to an enthusiastic campaign of sabotage and good-natured sparring. All-night street-riding sessions through New York City, long shifts behind the wheel of the rig, and highly charged freestyle shows would create an unforgettable ethos and atmosphere among the team members—all of whom had come to realize that times were changing. Nonetheless, home again in Leucadia at the end of the summer tour, Lee easily transitioned back into his daily routine.

After the '89 Tour of Kings, I was living at the Enchanted house with Kevin [Martin] and Joe [Johnson]. We would usually ride the ramp or some street spots in the morning, and then head to the beach in the afternoon. We were still riding school shows around the area and the King of Vert Finals were coming up, so I was riding the ramp a lot too.

Brad McDonald from Go magazine wanted to arrange to do a shoot with me on the Enchanted ramp, but the night before I had been out late drinking a lot of vodka. We had recently installed a metal coping rail, and during the shoot I did a Peg Grind and came right off the end of the ramp, trapping my leg in the front triangle and hearing a loud snap. I was about to sign a contract with Haro for the following year, but it went on hold because I wasn't able to ride. I went back to England to recover.

– Lee Reynolds

Reynolds's physical recovery in England gave him the opportunity to step back from the intensity of the freestyle world and consider his options. With the well-publicized decline in the BMX business beginning to take its toll on the international scene, the future of the sport was looking less assured than ever. Unable to ride, and watching many of his friends moving on to college and full-time jobs, Lee began to indulge other creative interests––music and DJ'ing in particular. Later, on his return to California in 1991, he would personally observe the extent of the industry meltdown. Nonetheless, a group of young amateurs including Jon Peacey, Bill Nitschke, Kurt Schmidt, and Danny Meng had kept the faith. As the new faces of the Haro team, they were competing in smaller regional contests such as the Hoffman Bicycle Stunt series and Randy Loop's King of Flatland event. Unfavorable market conditions had spelled the end of the glory days; large salaries and company credit cards had been replaced by product-flow deals or, at best, contest and travel expenses. But Reynolds reconnected with his friend and ex-Hutch teammate Chris Potts, and the two joined flatland specialist Ed Lenander for a year of freestyle shows for Haro at local venues.

I came back to California in 1991 and the scene around San Diego had almost vanished. Ron had sold the Enchanted house and moved south to Lemon Grove, and the vert scene had been pretty much replaced by street and dirt. I returned to Haro to ride in some local shows with Chris [Potts] and Ed [Lenander], but I was getting into DJ'ing and I just graduated to spending more time doing that and learning graphic design. They were great years. Sometimes it's hard to believe that I managed to break into that great '80s Haro team, as a kid who just decided to take a chance and move to California.

– Lee Reynolds

My big break in the magazines came when Tim Leighton Boyce and Nick Philip from RAD Magazine came to shoot some pictures of Greg Guillotte and me at Meanwhile Gardens Skate Park. I asked them why they didn't do the 'Me and my Bike' articles anymore in the magazine and they said, 'OK, let's do one with you.' I was beyond stoked!

Reynolds "Inverted" in early 1989 on the "Enchanted Ramp".

April 1991 - The Three bike weekend. Mat Hoffman
made numerous attempts to backflip the doubles at an
early 2Hip dirt contest, held at the Dirt Brothers, Mission
Trails set up in San Diego. Pictured here returning Chris
Pott's twisted Platinum colored '91 Haro Sport, having
run out of his trademark Air Master frames.

First it was Wilkerson who took the ball. Times
were changing fast and Ron stepped up and showed
how, with a commitment from one person, you could
totally change direction and re energize the sport. He
planted that seed with me. If you take a risk and make
it happen, people are going to follow you for the right
reasons and for the good of something that they truly
believe in. Then the money really got thin and it was
a case of running contests and losing money. That's
when I was dumb enough to step up and say 'All right,
I'll lose the money now,' and that's when I started to
figure out what I was going to do.

– Mat Hoffman

19 | THE HARO
RACE DIVISION

I took the role as race team manager for Haro at the beginning of 1985, when it was clear that we needed somebody to manage the numerous athlete commitments that we had within the ABA and NBL race scenes. At first the job involved traveling to races and making sure the guys had clean and well-presented plates and kits, although Bob maintained an interest in races and wanted to do more. At the time we had the best guys out there running kit and plates: Stu Thompson, Greg Hill, Harry Leary, Eddie King, Eric Rupe, and Gary Ellis, to name a few. These guys were all over the magazine covers and it was my job to make sure they looked good and got paid for the coverage. At the start of that season, Bob told me he was designing a race bike and that I should identify a rider who could win. He also pointed out that most of the race brands were launching freestyle bikes, so we should move into BMX race in a much bigger way. I was a good friend of Eddy King's, but I just felt that Pete Loncarevich should be our man. I felt that he was capable of winning all three titles in one year if we got it right, and that had never been done...

– Ron Haro

The arrival of Pro BMX Racer Pete Loncarevich at the ABA Grand National Finals in Oklahoma City in late 1985 was a remarkable moment in the success story of Haro Designs. Loncarevich's association with Haro appeared to be no different than that of his rivals; he had a deal to run a Haro plate, leathers, and gloves. But the arrangement that brought "Pistol Pete" to Oklahoma over Thanksgiving weekend began a controversial episode that would ultimately play out in Haro's favor.

Since November 1984, Bob Haro had watched with interest as almost every established brand in the BMX racing world set its sites on the rapidly expanding and highly lucrative freestyle market. Soon he would find himself in direct competition with old friends and acquaintances––men and women he had forged relationships and rubbed shoulders with at dusty, crowded race meetings across the length and breadth of the United States. With the appointment of his brother Ron Haro as team manager, and the acquisition of Loncarevich as the team's first professional factory rider, Bob Haro chose to fight fire with fire as he ventured into the established BMX race scene, fueled by the same ambition and focus that had launched the Haro brand into a leadership position in the freestyle market.

Although Haro Designs will always be more obviously linked to freestyle, Bob Haro's efforts to establish his new venture in the raw and highly progressive late 1970s BMX racing scene enabled the brand to grow from its humble beginnings. Haro's early involvement in the sport inspired him to design and create a series of innovative products that would not only improve the technology and performance of the basic hardware but also mark him within the scene as a respected designer and entrepreneur. As a teenager traveling with the ABA and NBL race circuit in the late 1970s and early 1980s (initially as a competitor; later to showcase freestyle riding), Bob Haro became an expert networker and a popular personality within the BMX racing world.

By 1983, Haro had developed a collection of dedicated products that would position the brand as the leading clothing and accessories supplier to the BMX racing scene. The Haro Racing label would account for almost every conceivable consumable or practical item required by a rider, from gear bags and number plates to leathers and gloves. A Haro racing bike, however, was conspicuously absent. With his widespread commitments and limited resources, Bob understood that he could not be a major player in the hardware business. Instead, he decided to work closely with the bike manufacturers in terms of branding and graphic design services, and provided heartfelt assurances that he had no interest in enticing riders away from their factory sponsors. This arrangement, largely based in trust, proved successful. As a result, Haro regularly enjoyed the sight of almost every elite pro BMX rider barreling toward him on the press-packed first berm of countless BMX races, adorned with the colors and branding of Haro Designs.

By 1985, Bob Haro had been lured away from the front line of the BMX racing scene by opportunities within the lucrative freestyle market. With his days of traveling the country to carefully prepare the number plates and kits of his prized co-sponsored athletes behind him, his younger brother Ron stepped up to the plate. Ron's duties were initially similar to those of his elder brother, but soon he became the eyes and ears of the Haro race set-up by reporting news and intelligence about the state of the scene and its top-performing athletes. Within a year of his new appointment, he would manage the brand's transition into a full-factory racing team.

"Pistol" Pete Loncarevich was born in April 1966, in Lake Forest, Orange County, California. The spectacular mountain ranges that surround OC were a popular venue and racing environment for the emerging West Coast motocross scene in the late 1960s and early 1970s. High-profile events, including the Lake Elsinore Grand Prix, drew the region's young families from their suburban neighborhoods into the hills to watch as the sport's young titans battled for honors in a haze of dust and blue smoke. As the early '70s MX scene inspired a generation of California kids to find an alternative way to compete and race on two wheels, the BMX movement began.

At 8 years of age, Pete received his first race bike: a Schwinn Stingray chopper-style machine that enabled him to start competing. He started racing at Elks BMX Lodge in Santa Ana, winning numerous amateur contests including the 1978 Corona National. Over the next two years, a series of encouraging results began to attract positive attention that resulted in co-sponsorship arrangements with a local BMX shop, Mulroney Schwinn; a formative BMX racing brand, Cook Brothers; and S&S (Steel and Strip) Performance products. His local success eventually paved the way for a series of high-profile opportunities, the first of which came in 1980 when Sandy Finkelman, team manager of the newly formed Diamond Back BMX race team, approached Loncarevich with an offer of factory sponsorship. After two successful years of racing for Diamond Back as an amateur ended due to a professional disagreement, Loncarevich felt ready to step up and compete in the professional ranks.

His sponsor, however, preferred to have him continue competing as an amateur and to set his sights on winning the National Team trophy. Loncarevich, however, entered the ABA Jag World Championships on December 29 in the pro division, where his second-place finish would not be celebrated by his sponsor. Within minutes of the race's conclusion, a representative from Diamond Back announced the termination of Pete's contract.

Loncarevich's departure from the Diamond Back team was soon followed by another exciting opportunity. Local BMX pioneer and entrepreneur Scott Breithaupt was made aware of Loncarevich's free status and invited him to join his SE racing factory team as a professional. Titan and legend of the sport Stu Thompson had helped Breithaupt establish the team by winning numerous professional titles through the late 1970s before moving on and joining the Redline factory team. SE was still a relatively small brand when Loncarevich joined in February of 1983; this arrangement would last for approximately one month, until Breithaupt became aware of the existence of a competitive sub-brand that Loncarevich had recently started with his father, called LRP (Loncarevich Racing Products). A short spell riding for Shadow Racing resulted in a successful three-year period with CW (Custom Works) Racing, beginning in December of 1983.

But the CW deal also began with the threat of controversy. Once again, the existence of the LRP brand was considered to be a conflict of interest. CW owner Roger Worsham stood

firm, stipulating that LRP be dissolved if Pete were to join as a fully sponsored factory pro; thus, in December of 1983, a deal was signed but LRP was no longer in operation. In May of 1983, Loncarevich tasted his first victory as a professional BMX racer. Victory in the "B" pro division, at the NBL War of the Stars in Northridge, California, unveiled the exciting potential that the young Californian brought to CW. On May 30, he climbed onto the podium for the second time within a month to collect a trophy for third place in his first senior category pro race at the ABA Spring Nationals in Freemont, California. In October of 1983, Loncarevich reached a major milestone by registering his first victory as a senior pro at the ABA Wheaties Gold Cup in Las Vegas, Nevada. The next 12 months would bring more success at pro level for Loncarevich and CW, who would complete and market the signature-model CW racing "Pistol Pete" frame. But with the sport booming in popularity and global participation continuing to grow, even larger sums of money would soon filter into the pro BMX racing ranks. As an ambitious 18-year-old rising star of the pro division, enjoying a rich vein of form, Pete Loncarevich would soon be on the move once again.

In early April of 1985, a telephone discussion between Loncarevich and Haro VP Jim Ford concluded with the scheduling of an imminent meeting at Haro's head office in Carlsbad to discuss sponsorship options for the upcoming season. Although some dialogue had taken place with Ron Haro, Loncarevich had prepared

The ABA Grand's, November, 1985, Oklahoma, L - R, Ron Haro, Pete Loncarevich and Bob Haro remind CW Racing's Roger Worsham that he has lost his star rider. In a blatant message to CW, the Jersey Loncarevich wears bares the slogan "April Fools". The message references the legal dispute escalated by CW in a bid to prevent Loncarevich from joining Haro before his loosely written contract ended in April.

I approached Pete at a race and soon after that he came down to Haro for a meeting. I was absolutely convinced that he would be perfect for the situation. We agreed on terms at the meeting in Carlsbad and were on our way. CW racing had heard rumors about the discussion and started to respond with threats of legal action, but Jim Ford and I had looked at Pete's contract and it had an early-release clause that he was within his rights to activate.

– Ron Haro

for what he considered to be a routine meeting with his co-sponsor to review his number plate and his glove deal. But Bob Haro and Jim Ford had a more ambitious idea. Although he was still racing for CW, Loncarevich's contract contained a loophole that could allow him to discuss terms elsewhere. At the request of his older brother, Bob, Haro Racing Team Manager Ron Haro had identified Loncarevich as a rider who could become the company's first professional racer–– one with enough potential to fast-track Haro to a strong position in the national race scene.

Loncarevich would return to CW soon after this meeting, to discuss his options with company owner Roger Worsham. Having secured the ABA Number One Pro title for 1984, the young pro was in the mood to make the best of his form and boost his earning power in a sport that offered, at best, few financial assurances. However, Worsham was outraged when he heard of Loncarevich's negotiation with Haro, and the situation quickly devolved into a legal dispute. Still, the sponsorship package on offer from Haro was significantly better than the arrangement with CW; moreover, Loncarevich was excited about the possibility of directly contributing to the geometry and design of the forthcoming Haro Group 1 race bike. Despite the restraining order initiated by CW, which specified that Loncarevich was under contract until April of 1986, their complaint failed in civil court. Legal action was dropped when, allegedly, it seemed unlikely that Loncarevich would secure the ABA Number One title for the second straight year. As a result, and he arrived at the ABA Grand National Finals in November wearing a Haro Designs race uniform. Haro had its man, who felt ready to capitalize on his good form and earning potential.

The formative Haro Factory Race Team stepped up for its full debut season in 1986. Two promising Californian amateur racers, Danny Milwee and Mike King, lined up alongside Loncarevich; together, the three riders would form a team that enabled Haro to compete in categories and age groups across the three main governing bodies (ABA, NBL, and USBA). As the original Haro pro racer, Loncarevich set off with a new-found focus on his first–– and most successful––year of his early BMX racing career. Cutting a formidable figure at the gate with a more-muscular physique, a deep appetite for success, and the stylish branded uniform of his sponsor, he dominated the podium of all three BMX racing organizations on a busy calendar of almost constant travel and competition. In his first full year at Haro, he became the first and last rider in the history of the sport to secure the NBL, USBA, and ABA pro titles in the same year. A landslide victory in the 1986 BMX reader-voted Racer of the Year poll; first place at the Murray World Cup in Nashville, Tennessee; and the coveted NORA (Number One Rider Award) Cup concluded this record-setting season.

Haro's phenominal success in the team's debut season must be credited, in part, to the vision of the management team of Bob and Ron Haro and Jim Ford. Loncarevich's success, of course, contributed another unique factor. But in addition, the two younger amateur riders, Mike King and Danny Milwee, had both settled into life at Haro and were beginning to make an impact. The next year would bring more success, more growth as a team, and a far more diverse landscape for competitive racing.

At the beginning of 1987, to categorically broaden appeal and transition older riders out of the plateauing BMX race scene, a new bicycle

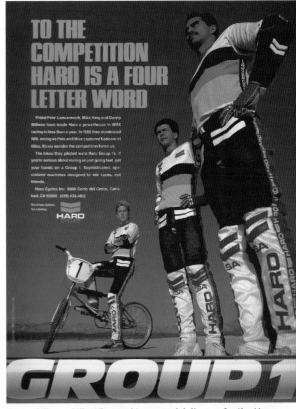

Danny Milwee, Mike King and Loncarevich line up for the Haro Racing Division's debut magazine advert.

Loncarevich in action with the Number 1 plate.

Bill Hawkins and Bob Haro observe the strength testing and alignment of a Haro race frame at Anlen in Taiwan.

We unveiled Pete as our rider, along with the new Haro Group 1 race bike at the ABA Grands in October of '85. I was pushing the new bike across the track and was stopped by Gary Ellis, a pro GT racer. He looked at it and said it was the best-looking bike he had ever seen. Bob and Pete had basically designed it between them and it had these amazing graphics.

– Ron Haro

appeared on the market. The F-1 was essentially a miniature road-racing bike, with derailleur gearing front and rear and frame geometry that could accommodate adult riders. The racing format quickly evolved into a mixture of multiple short laps on a course much like a road criterium course, but demonstrated with the frenetic and energetic style of BMX racing. The early F-1 scene benefitted from a significant marketing push, largely due to the backing of bicycle technology giant Shimano, but was unable to reach and identify a specific fan base. Soon, however, new and ambitious F-1 brands would throw caution to the wind and pitch their best riders into the mix.

In a series of staged races regulated by the NBL and AFA and populated by rival BMX brands––including Diamond Back and Hutch

Hi-Performance––Loncarevich and Mike King rode the dedicated Haro Dart F-1. Because Haro was also attempting to infiltrate the burgeoning mountain-bike scene, King and Loncarevich, along with female amateur Tara Llanes, agreed to represent the company at a series of races held in throughout the California mountains. Loncarevich went on to win the Vision Street Wear World Cup (formerly the Murray World Cup, which he had taken home the year before), as well as the coveted BMX Plus! Racer of the Year readers' poll, but endured a frustrating conclusion to the '87 season when he sustained a broken collarbone while racing at the ABA Regional World Cup in Reno, Nevada. Although he attempted to speed up the estimated three-month recovery period by seeking private treatment, his goal of racing competitively at the ABA Grands Finals five weeks later would see him underprepared and unable to pass the

semifinals of the pro division. Another debilitating injury, this time two broken ribs while training, set him back another month and banished any remaining end-of-season ambitions.

Pete Loncarevich, one of the most competitive and successful BMX racers of all time, propelled Haro into the sport's upper echelons with his timely arrival at the company and his record-setting first full season as the original member of the Haro Factory Race Team. After bringing immediate and long-lasting credibility and respect to his sponsor, in 1989 he underwent a brief period of disillusionment and briefly retired. His re-emergence, with sponsorship from the Vans shoe brand, unleashed another fantastic period of domination that saw two more BMX national titles and a second competitive career, this time as a downhill mountain-bike racer. Pete Loncarevich is a legend of our sport.

Loncarevich "Cleared up" in his first full season with Haro taking the ABA, USBA and NBL National number one titles.

That was the last year for the USBA, and as far as I know, no other rider has ever held all three titles in one year. Each month I would send Pete an envelope that contained a Haro Number 1 decal for his plate. There was nothing else, not even a note. It was my way of supporting and motivating him in a season where he just killed it. He would have been World Champion too that year, but we opted to race in the domestic series over the weekend of the Worlds event in Seattle. Pete wanted the points to secure the three titles. And it paid off.

– Ron Haro

In a crowded freestyle market, the RSI, Group 1 Race bike became a statement of intent from Haro Designs.

As the Huffy race team disbanded, it made sense for their star rider to escalate his co sponsorship to a factory deal with Haro Designs. And King would not disappoint.

21 | MIKE KING

The arrival of promising amateur BMX racer Mike King in early 1986 was an unexpected bonus for the newly formed Haro racing division. Team manager Ron Haro, already delighted with the capture of emerging pro racer Pete Loncarevich from rival brand CW Racing in October of '85, welcomed King and a 14-year-old Californian named Danny Milwee. Together, they would enable Haro to unleash a legitimate factory team into the 1986 NBL and ABA national race serie's. Through a fiercely competitive season, both riders rose to the challenge and established the Haro racing division as a compact yet formidable new force.

Mike King was born in Washington, D.C., on June 30, 1969. When he was barely six months old, the King family relocated to San Diego, where both Mike and his older brother Eddy would grow up embracing the outdoor lifestyle and climate. In the mid-1970s the two found a second home at the Silver Wing BMX Track, near Montgomery Park in San Diego, and began racing their department- store BMX bikes in the raw and spirited local scene. By 1975, 12-year-old Eddy had gained some local recognition, including a modest but legitimate sponsorship deal with S & W Bike in San Diego. In 1979, at 10 years of age, Mike followed in his brother's footsteps with an arrangement to represent Wheels'n'Things, a El Cajon-based bike shop owned by Sandy Finkelman (who would later become Diamond Back team manager).

In the mid-1980s, King capped an amateur career punctuated by long periods away from the racetrack by becoming prominent in the US National BMX racing scene. Although he raced throughout the early decade, he preferred to compete in the local NBA district 'S' Division in San Diego and was rarely seen at national events. Despite his fluctuating commitment to racing, King remained respected and competitive. Then in March of 1983, after three years of loyally racing for and representing the Diamond Back team, the now-19-year-old Eddy King signed a professional contract and joined seasoned AA pro racers Harry Leary and Pete Loncarevich as a senior rider. At 13, younger brother Mike quickly became motivated to follow a similar path and focused on obtaining a contract of his own; by 1984, he would be named the ABA's number one amateur racer. Next, a short stint of racing for Bicycle Parts Pacific, the company that resurrected the failed late-1970s Dirt Slinger brand, set King up for his first genuine factory sponsorship.

In March 1984, King departed Dirt Slinger for a support-team role with the highly successful and respected Redline Engineering team. Within 10 days, however, 15-year-old Mike King had accepted a lucrative and more committed offer to join the well-financed Huffy BMX racing team––which had recently renewed its BMX ambitions by signing number one pro racer Stuart Thomson. In his new position, King would secure the amateur NBL and ABA National Number One titles over consecutive years. But despite this swift rise to success, in late 1985 Huffy made an abrupt exit from BMX racing after the ABA Grands, leaving King and his teammates to contemplate their future options.

Huffy disbanded [its racing team] in late 1985 and I joined the new Haro racing team almost immediately. It felt like a natural transition for me since Haro had sponsored the Huffy team. I was also very familiar with Bob, his brother Ron, and the other employees. The Haro offices were just a 30-minute drive north from our home and I had just received my driver's license that summer, so I made an effort to drive up and see these guys at least once a week.

– Mike King

With the arrival of Mike King, Haro was able to line up a three-man racing team for the 1986 season. Pete Loncarevich, the team's pro contender, immediately embarked upon a record-setting season of almost total domination; through the busy calendar year, he secured the NBA, NBL, and USBA titles to become the number-one pro rider in the world. This alone was enough to make Haro the number- one team in its debut season. But in addition, the team's younger amateur, Danny Milwee, began the year on a probationary deal that became a permanent sponsorship arrangement after a series of excellent results. Continuing from where he had left off with Huffy, King raced and won consistently and steadily moved toward his ultimate goal of becoming Haro's second pro-class racer. In 1987, over a season in which he seemingly had little left to prove outside the pro ranks, he showed beyond all doubt that he was the most exciting amateur rider in the world. In his final year as an amateur, he was crowned IBMXF Supercross World Champion as well as the Vision Streetwear World Champion, he also took the premier NBL and ABA number-one titles for a fourth consecutive year.

Bob [Haro]'s friend Bob Hadley called to let us know that the Huffy team was disbanding after the 1985 ABA Grands and that Mike King would be available. Mike was winning everything as an amateur but after a chat with Jim Ford about potentially signing him, Jim was convinced that we couldn't afford it. But Bob agreed that we needed to have him on the team, as he was the number- one amateur In the country and we were ambitious. Pete Loncarevich had already introduced us to Danny Milwee, who was young, and his father was helping with costs, so Mike came in and became our third rider.

– Ron Haro

I won the ABA and NBL number-one titles in 1987 and felt like I had accomplished everything I had set out to do as an amateur. Technically, I turned pro in 1988, but the NBL season started in the fall of 1987 so my debut pro race was the Christmas Classic in Columbus, Ohio. I started racing in the 'A' pro ranks, which was the mandatory pro-rookie class that new pros competed in until they had earned $5,000 in prize money. The team dynamic at Haro was great. Pete had previously ridden for Diamond Back and was a teammate of my older brother Eddy, so I knew him well before we became teammates. He taught me a lot, as did my older brother, who was highly motivated for me to train hard and to realize my potential. I was lucky to have an older brother to look up to for support and advice when I made the step up.

– Mike King

King's entry into the professional ranks started in the best possible way. A series of blistering performances quickly elevated the 18-year-old rookie out of the 'A' Pro class and into the realm of the sport's elite competitors. In his first AA pro event, the Northwest Nationals in Vancouver, Washington, he announced his arrival in explosive style by winning all four main-event pro races in a single weekend. This first opportunity to test himself and to compete against the established elite riders of the 'AA' pro ranks altered the dynamic and hierarchy of the professional sport. King, who would continue to dominate throughout the 1988 season, finished his rookie year as the ABA's number one 'AA' pro racer.

My main motivations for turning pro were the challenge and opportunity to race against the best riders in the world but also to race against my older brother. After three pro nationals, I was eligible to race against the big boys, the AA pros, and at the Northwest Nationals in Vancouver and I won all four pro races. This was probably one of my proudest career moments in BMX, especially winning the number one title in my rookie year.

– Mike King

The arrival of F-1 Bicycle racing in the late 1980s initiated a bizarre new category of racing that ultimately became nothing more than a distraction to the BMX world. The futuristic format, which was based on racing bicycles that utilized the technology, gearing and geometry of traditional road bikes - but with a 20-inch wheel size - initially appealed to many of the elite BMX racers. In 1987, Haro designed and released its own dedicated F-1 model, the Dart. Over the remainder of the decade, both Mike King and Pete Loncarevich would experiment with the new sport; however, the perceived similarities between BMX and F-1 would prove untenable. The long-distance racing format, unfortunately, required the transitioning BMX racers to trade their explosive power for endurance––a realization that would contribute to the new sport's demise.

The F-1 bike and the race series was something that a few established BMX companies invested into, and I had no reason not to try it. At first, several top pro riders wanted to experiment with this new type of racing but later found how tough it was once everyone understood that you needed to have a solid base of endurance training. At that age, I thought I was invincible and that my pain threshold could cope with it but I later found out (along with many others who competed) that it was a very different type of racing. In the end, it was merely a big learning experience that didn't pan out after two or three years.

– Mike King

In 1990, King was justufiably rated as one the most competitive pro BMX racers in the world. A naturally ambitious individual, he soon began to look further into the future, where he would seek new opportunities to capitalize on his success, winning mentality, and vast experience.

King found form immediately for Haro and continued to dominate through his transition to AA Pro.

A chance conversation at the Interbike trade show resulted in an opportunity to utilize these skills even as it also spelled the end of his five-year association with Haro. The career of his good friend and rival, Redline's AA pro racer Billy Griggs would advance as well.

At the start of the 1990 season, friends and race rivals Mike King and Billy Griggs traded places as riders from opposing teams. Griggs completed successful negotiations with Bob Haro in Carlsbad, while Mike King headed to Redline, Griggs's former team, as team manager and AA pro racer. King spent three years at Redline before a brief spell at the Balance Bicycle team and GT; there, he enjoyed a successful era racing mountain bikes in the downhill and dual slalom in the NORBA and UCI professional ranks; in 1993, he was crowned the UCI Mountain Bike Downhill world Champion and in 1994 and 1995, he became the ABA's pro cruiser champion. In 1999, King returned to Haro Designs as an established and seasoned mountain-bike racer. His contribution to the sport of BMX earned him induction into the BMX Hall of Fame that same year.

After five years with Haro I started to look at extending my role to that of team manager while also continuing to race in the pro class. Chuck Hooper at Redline had expressed an interest in creating a similar role at Redline after a discussion at Interbike that year, and things started to fall into place in late December. I finished the year as ABA number four and Billy was having a great year…he almost won the pro title. I think Haro knew I was exploring my market value, so when they had an opportunity to sign Billy they pulled the trigger and it turned out to be a win-win for both of us.

I had some of the best years riding for Haro and I was very pleased to win both amateur and pro titles within my first two years on the team.

– Mike King

It was late September, and I can't remember who actually called me…it might have been Jim, Brad, or Dean Bradley…but they said they had managed to get things sorted out and they were free of Derby Cycle. They had a limited with budget but they were able to get me back onto a BMX and pick up where we had left off. I went back and they had the first-generation Monocoque race frame that Linn was making from aluminum. It had this amazing joint at the head tube, it was a bitchin'-looking bike. It was a big improvement from the two-piece composite frame they had in 1992.

– Billy Griggs

Grigg's immediately found himself as the senior Pro racer at Haro following his arrival.

22 | BILLY GRIGGS

In the late 1970s, the "Y" BMX Track in Orange, Southern California, became the nucleus for a BMX movement that would go on produce some of the most talented riders in the history of the sport. After opening its gates for the first time in the summer of 1977, the Y drew huge crowds from the heartland of the emerging industry over long weekends and through a packed weeknight schedule that would enable local kids to rise to the challenge and find the competitive fire within. One of those kids was 13-year-old Billy Griggs. Born in the city of Anaheim in Orange County, his journey into the tempestuous early world of competitive BMX racing began in an ordinary suburban neighborhood with a group of like-minded friends and neighbors.

I started racing because all the neighborhood knuckleheads who had BMX bikes were building jumps and terrorizing the neighborhood. My dad put me on a motorcycle at 2-and-a-half years old but he was a long-haul truck driver so I didn't get to develop my motorcycle-riding skills as much as I would have liked. So I would ride my BMX bike and do whatever I could to make it feel like I was on the motorcycle until my dad got home. In December of 1980, we had been away for the holidays at my grandmother's house on the East Coast, and when we got back after New Year's a lot of the kids I had been riding with had gotten these new BMX bikes for Christmas. My buddies were all telling me about the Orange 'Y' BMX Track in Anaheim and everybody had signed up to race. I went out and there with my friends and my bike and I never looked back.

– Billy Griggs

Following a series of promising results in the beginner class at the Y, Griggs secured his first taste of sponsorship. At BS Bikes, a shop owned and operated by freestyle pioneer and GT team manager Brian Scura on Harbor Boulevard in the nearby city of Santa Ana, Griggs joined a group of talented local youngsters who would eventually race in the BS jersey. A stint of a few weeks with Santa Ana-based Bassett Racing toward the end of 1982 led to a deal with the high-profile CW racing brand, where Griggs would rise through the ranks of the ABA and begin to make a name for himself as a talented amateur racer.

In 1983, a factory deal with CW was a pretty big deal. They supplied me with bikes and parts and covered all of the event expenses. If we won the team trophy, there would usually be some prize money that would be dispersed among all of the riders. It took the financial burden off my parents for bike parts and travel, which allowed them to travel and support me.

– Billy Griggs

The CW deal launched Griggs into a period of ascendancy in which he displayed a more-focused approach to racing in recognition of the responsibilities of representing a factory brand. However, in a year in which he would win the 15 Expert National Amateur title, he also became disillusioned with CW's reluctance to discuss and produce a bike with a more suitable geometry for his size and physique. Instead, CW's Roger Worsham preferred to design a bike for Griggs that featured a unique 'Z' feature in the down tube, a design that added weight to the frame and caused Griggs much frustration.

The Z frame was one of the most ridiculous ideas I had ever seen. It wasn't lighter, and it wasn't stronger; it was purely a gimmick to set it apart and create sales. They made some efforts to produce one with a custom head angle and improved geometry but I was never really very excited about riding it. I liked faster steering and more aggressive geometry, so that frame was a step backwards from what I needed.

– Billy Griggs

In January of 1984, following a mixed but ultimately successful season, Billy Griggs decided to leave CW and join the newly appointed Schwinn Factory Team. Schwinn had been alerted to the growth in BMX racing and was in the process of mounting an ambitious assault on the market with a new range of bikes and accessories. Once again disillusioned by the lack of interest in producing a competitive bike with a suitable geometry, Griggs decided to take matters into his own hands. At CW he had raced on the frame of a rival brand that was decorated with CW decals. With this frame in hand, he approached expert frame designer Voris Dixon and within a week was riding the new frame at a national event. But Schwinn would prove difficult to convince of the benefits of the specification; instead, the company focused on the statement of defiance that Griggs was making by unlawfully producing his own frame to look almost exactly like a Schwinn Predator. Differences between the 15-year-old expert racer and Schwinn management would prove irreconcilable. After six months on the team, Griggs resigned and began to consider his next move.

The early 90's race scene was a colorful and competitive place. Although the sport was enduring hard times, the show would go on thanks to sponsors like GT and Haro.

I got a call from their office questioning why, as a 16-year-old amateur, I was being paid to race. They changed my deal on the spot, offering travel costs and expenses but stating that I would no longer get paid a salary to ride as an amateur on the team. I could have turned pro at that point, but I wanted to do it on my terms and not be forced into it too early. And actually they didn't even offer me that opportunity. They just made it clear they wouldn't pay a rider who was an amateur and that was that.

– Billy Griggs

In response to his demotion, Griggs made arguably the most important move of his amateur career when he began negotiations in late 1985 with Steve Giberson, the newly appointed Race Team Manager of Redline Engineering. Within a week, he had moved seamlessly across Chatsworth to join the Redline team. The next year, 1986, Griggs and new pro recruit Greg Hill would become the sole representatives of the Redline Race Team.

Schwinn made the sting frame, but it just didn't suit my riding style. It was a beautifully made bike from a fabrication point of view but the geometry was awful for me with a super-low bottom bracket and a 5-inch head tube. There had been some discussions about me coming to Chicago to work on a frame with an engineer but even though I kept raising the question, and losing races, it never materialized. So I decided to deal with the problem myself. It was a case of making my point to Schwinn, but they just told me I couldn't ride it as it wasn't Schwinn-approved and if I kept riding it they would have to let me go…and so it was. I just wanted to win races and I didn't want to get a reputation for being the guy that kept changing teams, so I considered riding as a privateer for the rest of the season.

– Billy Griggs

His departure from Schwinn would lead Griggs to the legendary Mongoose BMX products in Chatsworth, north of Los Angeles. There had been loose discussions between Mongoose team manager Brett Allen and Griggs shortly after the latter had joined Schwinn, with Allen expressing disappointment over not having known about Griggs's desire to leave CW. Within days the two were meeting at company headquarters to discuss the possibility of Griggs joining the team. Mongoose had local manufacturing resources and also understood the need for its riders to have frames that suited their builds and racing styles. Griggs agreed to join the brand, effective immediately; within weeks he was lining up at a national ABA race on a modified Mongoose Californian race bike. But this unsettling and turbulent period in his amateur career was far from over, and cruel circumstances would bring about the end of Mongoose arrangement. Owner and president Skip Hess decided to sell the company and its assets; in 1986, the vast American Recreation Group would acquire the Mongoose brand. With a new executive group in charge, it wasn't long before budgets were scrutinized and Griggs received a call.

I had thought about turning pro but Linn wasn't keen and was very frank about his reasons for hiring me to be the 17-and-Under Expert rider. I was getting ready to graduate high school and was thinking about what I was going to do, keep racing or go to college. I decided I wanted to turn pro, which went against Linn's wishes but it was so up in the air as to what was going to happen because Seattle Bike Supply had expressed an interest in buying the brand. Linn had lost Greg and RL and I was the last marketable thing he had by way of a premier, named rider. I raced the first couple of races of 1987 as an expert but I had watched a few other guys in my expert class turn pro and I needed to be in that group. I raced the rest of 1987 as a pro and did pretty well. The guys at SBS who eventually took over were cool and positive, but the brand image was changing and I wasn't that excited about where they were taking it.

– Billy Griggs

Haro's entrance into the BMX racing scene with a genuine factory team line-up in 1986 had been a bold and unpredictable move. With almost every professional and known amateur racer in the national scene engaged in some form of co-sponsorship, Haro had cornered and dominated the non-bicycle side of the race market with a range of stylish and innovative parts and accessories. However, the company's transformation from nonthreatening collaborator to genuine competitor had caused a stir; in a volatile and highly competitive market, almost every competing factory team quickly outlawed the use of Haro accessories by their sponsored team riders. Haro's response was to field a small but highly competitive race team throughout the late 1980s.

But after a successful three-year period, the team's senior pro riders, Pete Loncarevich and Mike King, would become unsettled and leave the team. Haro would have to reinvent and repopulate its BMX racing program with new talent.

In late 1990, Griggs raced at the ABA Grands in Oklahoma City and although he didn't win his class, his performance made an impression. Like freestyle, BMX racing was experiencing a steady decline in participation at local levels. The national scene had maintained its intensity and large attendances, but the grassroots side of the sport was looking far less healthy. Griggs had placed well in his first three seasons in the pro ranks for Redline, and following a typically hard-fought and spirited performance in Oklahoma he received an unexpected telephone call.

I got a phone call from Bob Haro shortly after the ABA Grand's in 1990, completely out of the blue. He just asked me point-blank if I had any interest in coming to ride for Haro. My initial thought was that they had a great pro in Pete and Mikey had turned pro in '87. I was a really good friend of Mikey King's; as amateurs we didn't race against each other because I was five months older. In 1989 and 1990 we traveled together a lot. I was the only guy riding for Redline and he was the only guy riding for Haro and when we turned pro, we did race against each other. We never fell out or had cross words, though, even after the most heated races. So then Bob tells me he is calling me because Mikey is leaving and the slot is open and I would be the first choice to fill it. He had seen me race at the Grand's and liked the competitive approach that he saw from me. That's what he was looking for on his team

– Billy Griggs

Only a few weeks later, Griggs was seated in the Haro head office in Carlsbad negotiating the first of two individual contracts that would see him represent Haro as a pro racer in the 1990s. Following a discussion about frame geometries, Bob Haro gave Griggs his blessing to approach his previous employer, Linn Kastan, to discuss a solution. The idea was to position him for the next season on the most competitive gemoetry possible. The conversation was both surreal and rewarding, considering the history between the two.

Bob invited me down, we went to lunch, and we talked about what they wanted to do and what kind of program they liked to incentivize their riders with. It was a really easy decision for me. I liked where the brand was positioned; I liked that they had produced two ABA number-one titles with their previous two riders; and it just seemed like a winning brand. I recall Bob coming to the ABA Grands at the end of my first year with Haro. I was in the points and able to compete for the title mathematically. There was just such a feeling of support when Bob was at a race. Even though I missed out, we went out and had dinner and some drinks and I must say missed that the following year when he had left the brand.

– Billy Griggs

In the 1991 national race season, Griggs lined up as the senior rider for the Haro factory race team. A new group of young riders would also line up to represent the brand, including young amateur Larry Cambra, Cruiser specialist Kiyomi Waller, and a fearless 13-year-old female racer named Tara Llanes. Griggs' style and tenacity on the track set an example for his young amateur teammates. As the season unfolded, the potential and spirit among the group was plain to see. However, their potential also brought a moment of realization: if Haro were to close the gap and compete with the dominant GT, Powerlite, and Robinson teams, the company would need to invest. Therefore in early 1992, in collaboration with parts-and-accessories entrepreneur Don Crupi, the Haro - Crupi Race Team was formed. Griggs would go on to represent Haro as a factory pro in 1991, before a brief spell riding for the Iron Horse mountain-bike brand. But within a few months, under new circumstances, Griggs was back at Haro discussing terms for a new era. Haro had new owners, and a will to pick up where it had left off a few months earlier, so Billy Griggs would once again pull on the hallowed jersey of Haro Designs.

The day I signed my contract was awesome because Bob Haro was there. Riding for the team as a 13-year-old kid was an absolute dream come true. I loved every minute of being a bike racer.

– Tara Llanes

23 | TARA LLANES

In December of 1990, 14-year-old Californian Tara Llanes became the first female rider to join the Haro BMX Racing Team. Born in the neighborhood of West Covina, Los Angeles, and raised in a suburban neighborhood in Fullerton, Orange County, Llanes's introduction to the sport of BMX racing had begun just three years earlier. During a routine trip across town, 11-year-old Tara convinced her mother, Barbara, to stop the car as it passed the notorious "Y" BMX Track in Orange where a weekend of full-on racing was underway. This first taste of BMX left a lasting impression on the youngster; a week later she would return to the Y with her powder-blue Huffy BMX and an appetite to race.

By early 1988, Llanes was immersed in the local scene and had signed up as a privateer to race in the ABA's California District 3 division. Her first full season brought success at both local and district levels with regular top-three placements, and by early '89 she had attracted her first sponsorship arrangement with the Aussie Wear BMX Racing Team. This full debut year would establish the intrepid 12-year-old as a rising star in the sport, where she quickly gained a reputation as a fearless and focused young racer who liked to jump on her bike. By the end of her first full year she passed another milestone by taking her first national victory in the 12 Girls Division at the ABA Super Nationals in Jenks, Oklahoma. Her

consistent performances throughout the 1989 race season would both position her as the Number Two rider nationally in the 12 and Under BMX and Cruiser class and, inevitably, garner the interest and attention of the established factory teams.

I think initially it was Billy Griggs who gave the guys at Haro my name, but at the same time I had started consistently placing in the top three. Billy and I and I both trained at the Orange 'Y' BMX track and when I was about 13 or 14 he became a bit of a coach and mentor to me, as well as good friend. Haro wanted to expand and have a full team presence instead of just a solo pro rider as they had done in the past. So they signed Billy Griggs as the pro, Kiyomi Waller as the top cruiser guy, myself as the girl, and Larry Cambra as the younger amateur rider.

– Tara Llanes

A trip to Carlsbad to sign contracts and meet the Haro staff brought Tara face to face with company president Bob Haro. An arrangement to bring the teenager on board was made, and within a few weeks she was in action for her new sponsor. Throughout the year she would dominate her division, and finish the season off with 1990 number-one titles at district and national levels. In addition, she was also crowned the Girls Grand National ChaChampion in Oklahoma City late in the year.

El Paso, Texas
SUPERNATIONALS
APRIL 3, 4, 5, 1992

Llanes found her calling immediately in the BMX race scene in California.

The formation of the joint Haro/Crupi BMX racing team in early 1992 brought more new faces to the team. In response to the dominance of the GT factory team and their established umbrella brands, Powerlite and Robinson, Haro and parts-and-accessories manufacturer Crupi formed an alliance in order to capitalize on their joint resources. Continuing her rich vein of form, Llanes once again dominated the 14 Girls Cruiser category, winning the ABA Silver Dollar Nationals in Reno, Nevada, in January and concluding her BMX racing years for Haro by securing number-one titles at district level in both 1991 and 1992. She would also secure the coveted NBL Grand National Champion title in 1992.

The year 1993 became one of transition for 16-year-old Tara Llanes when she was presented with an opportunity to put her skills to the test in a challenging new environment. Mountain-bike racing had grown rapidly through the late 1980s; predictably, a number of the established BMX brands had recognized and responded to the chance to break into the vibrant new sport. This process was aided by mountain-bike guru Dean Bradley, who had joined Haro in early 1987. His extensive knowledge of the developing scene had helped to accelerate the company through a learning curve that began with a series of off-the-shelf "all-terrain" bikes and persisted both through the development of a full-suspension model and into the precarious era of manufacturing frames and componentry from aluminum. To capture feedback and gain presence within the burgeoning off-road scene, Haro had begun to pitch its established BMX racers into various disciplines of the developing sport from as early as 1988. For her part, Tara Llanes would embrace the new challenge with typical dedication and commitment.

Llanes's transition from twenty-inch BMX Racing, to Mountain bike racing, was almost seamless. One of her many NORBA podium's.

Her mountain-bike-racing debut at Big Bear was a milestone for both the Haro brand and their young female racer. Seemingly unfazed by the transitional challenges between the two disciplines, Llanes would claim victory in the Junior Women's Dual Slalom at Big Bear—a pivotal moment in her bicycle-racing career. Her transformation from junior BMX racer to genuine contender in the packed ranks of the female NORBA (National Off-Road Bicycle Association) mountain-bike scene continued to evolve and unfold as she won silver and bronze medals at consecutive Winter X-Games and individual national titles in the Downhill, Dual Slalom, and Pro 4-Cross racing disciplines. This unmatched two-year period of results would position Llanes as one of the top female amateurs in the sport. Not surprisingly, in early 1996 she stepped up to compete in the professional world of mountain-bike racing. Often credited as a female BMX racer who could out-jump the boys, Llanes brought a more exciting dynamic to the girls' division of the early 1990s,

Tara Llanes represented Haro Designs through the formative years of her bicycle-racing career before signing professional contracts with a series of innovative brand leaders within the established mountain-bike industry. Unsuprisingly, she headed for, and made her home, in the mountain bike capital of the United States..

I graduated High School and moved to Durango, Colorado, which ended up being one of the best decisions of my life. Once I moved there I really felt like I was living the lifestyle because there were so many big name Pro's living there at the time, and I was able to just go ride with them. Missy, Elke, Ned, It was sort of like living in this crazy dream world. I mean I had just graduated High School and was living on my own and riding my bike every day for a living. It was just mind blowing!

– Tara Llanes

A lot of BMXers were transitioning into mountain-bike racing and doing well straight away. I think it was Brad Lusky who first asked me if I'd like to try getting on a mountain bike—I was definitely game. My first big race was the national at Big Bear, which was huge at the time. I remember I kept dropping my chain. I had never used a shifter/derailleur before and I just wasn't getting it. So after I'd dropped it like five times, I just put it in a gear and kept it there for the entire race!

– Tara Llanes

When I first started racing mountain bikes for Haro I just fell in love with the sport, the people, and the atmosphere. Our team changed through the years but my teammates on Haro were Michael 'Boom Boom' Bohannon, Phil Tinstman, and our XC guy Greg Marini A typical race weekend at a NORBA event almost felt like a local race because they were just super-chilled and so much fun. I loved the training, I always practiced the courses and got my lines down, and then on race day you've gotta just turn your brain off and go!

– Tara Llanes

With the support of her mom Barbara, Llanes travelled the ABA circuit and evolved into a bike racer.

The Haro fusion, and later Haro/Crupi Team enabled young local riders to develop their skills. Many would go onto success in the National BMX Racing scene.

The Haro Fusion Team relaxes between Moto's

Tara Llanes gets the most from her rental car.

24 | HARO RACE DIVISION INC. CONCLUSION

As the Haro Racing Division continued to evolve and expand through the early 1990s, its collaboration with Crupi granted both brands a more expansive presence within the national BMX racing scene. A talented group of young riders represented Haro across a broad range of age groups and disciplines. Many of them would transition into mountain bike racing, where they forged successful careers and became competitive athletes. In 1990, Cruiser specialist Kiyomi Waller became a teammate with Mike King, one of the most successful and stylish BMX racers of the late 1980s. During Waller's second spell with Haro in the 1997 and 1998 seasons, he twice secured the ABA National title in the highly competitive Cruiser category. Other young racers who represented Haro in the early 1990s included future brand manager Tony Degollado as well as Nick Thomson, Mike Luna, Andy Contes, Chris Acacia, Larry Cambra, and George Andrews. All helped to establish Haro Designs as a genuine BMX racing brand during the sport's most challenging era.

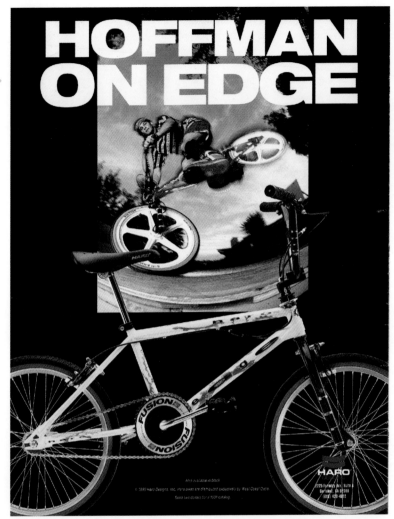

HOFFMAN ON EDGE

Hoffman "Nose Picks" on a budget freestyle model named the Haro "Edge".

When Bob and I put the deal together with West Coast Cycle, they understood us and how we had become successful, and to their credit they wanted to do it right. We were going to remain in Carlsbad and we were negotiating the future direction of the brand from a position of strength. But when Raleigh came along and bought West Coast, we lost that control because their interests and priorities lay in their crown jewel, which was the Raleigh brand. The end result was that we were kicked down another level when we actually needed even more support.

– Jim Ford

25 | 1990 - 1993

NEON WILDERNESS

As the BMX freestyle industry continued to adapt to the hardships of a lifeless market, many were left to contemplate the plight of the sport and its future direction. The riding scene of the late '80s had plowed headlong through a period of unrelenting and courageous innovation. The professional riders, and their fan base, had become obsessed with a single objective; the legacy of their lifestyle and the progression of their art, This evolved lifestyle enabled the older, more ambitous and independent riders to exert their own unique influence on the image of freestyle, and this dynamic that would play a direct role in defining the future identity of BMX.

As a result, the early '90s freestyle BMX landscape differed greatly from the highly marketable formula that had brought the sport to its zenith in the mid-1980s, when the industry had spawned and harvested a multi-million-dollar global market. The abrupt and largely unforeseen collapse of that market in 1989, however, had forced the brands to consolidate and diversify; by 1991, most were either out of the freestyle business or on life support.

The challenges at Haro HQ in Carlsbad in 1991 were not dissimilar, but a succession of ownership changes in the late 1980s had added to the company's burden of survival. Its management team of Bob Haro, Jim Ford, Brad Lusky, and Dean Bradley was now operating from an unfamiliar and frustrating position, largely driven by the surprise 1988 acquisition and merger of Haro's parent company West Coast Cycle, with a holding company named Derby Cycle International, who had recently acquired the Raleigh Worldwide brand from Seattle based Huffy. West Coast had bought Haro to leverage their highly successful national bicycle and accessory distribution network and had chosen to retain both Haro and Ford in senior management positions to ensure the future prosperity of the brand.

Nonetheless, both West Coast and Raleigh's new parent company were about to settle on a different set of priorities. Derby preferred to capitalize on the impressive West Coast Cycle distribution network to establish a fast and effective route to market for their exciting new prospect; Raleigh.

Mat Hoffman turns a "Lookdown" at the 2Hip King of Vert Thrasher land Finals in Phoenix, AZ.

Derby was trying to decide at senior level where Haro fit within their brand lineup, which included Raleigh, Cycle Pro, Nishiki, and us. It was largely taken out of our hands. We were a small California boutique style 20-inch brand that sold low volumes in a declining market and they couldn't figure out what we were going to become within their business, so we never really received a lot of help during that period of indecision. We knew that we wanted to continue being an innovative brand, but they were pushing for lower-end bikes and higher [sales] volumes.

– Dean Bradley

This shift left Haro propping up the pecking order within the Derby brand portfolio, which also included the road cycling and mountain-bike brand Nishiki and bicycle-component brand Cycle Pro (both acquired by Derby along with West Coast) Cycle. With BMX sales almost nonexistent in the late 1980's, and the Haro management team fending off calls to eradicate BMX in favor of diversification towards a more specialized mountain-bike line, the actions and decisions taken between 1991 and 1993 would be critical to the future of the Haro brand.

The year 1991 also saw significant changes in the leadership at the company. In his capacity as president, Bob Haro had become frustrated by the limitations placed on the company by the Derby regime; a constant battle had been waged to protect the brand and its unique image by the small Haro management team. Under the constant threat of being absorbed into the Derby operational set-up in the Pacific Northwest, Bob Haro began to consider walking away from the company he had founded and built from his bedroom, as a teenager, in the late 1970s. Now operating from what had essentially become a sales and marketing office in Carlsbad, Haro regularly repelled the efforts of Derby executives to interfere with the creative identity of the brand and its products. As high-level changes continued in the Derby hierarchy, the prospect of regular meetings with "a bunch of suits" at the Derby head offices in Washington State filled Haro, Ford, Bradley, and Luskey with dread. The idea of relocating to the Derby head office in Washington State was inconceivable.

The decline in freestyle interest also took its toll outside the company boardrooms. With almost non-existent marketing budgets, a high proportion of the leading factory teams had

Derby hired two marketing gurus to try to establish the most effective growth and promotion plan for the business, but they knew nothing about the BMX market. They didn't understand the history and pride of the Haro brand and where it had come from. We were a premium 20-inch brand, with a reputation as the leaders in the marketplace. The guys who came in, who were very well qualified as marketers, were trying to turn us into the opposite of that in search of higher [sales] volumes. The budgets were stripped away and there were no more teams and tours…they just didn't understand us as an image- based brand. It was all about price point and us being more of a commodity provider to a market that was alien to where we had come from. There was a lot of resistance and disagreement about the future direction of the brand and protecting Haro's unique history. So we fought back, because we didn't want to become an image-less brand.

– Brad Lusky

In late 1991, during the sprocket-jockey shows down at the Texas State Fair, Mat Hoffman mentioned to me that he was looking to put on a contest series. One of the things changing around that time was that skate parks were appearing in different regions of the country; we would regularly ride at Jeff Philipps' skate park in Texas after shows. There were now places you could hold a contest without having to drag a ramp across the country. As I recall, the 2Hip contests had finished because the budget disappeared when Vision pulled out and it was impossible to make it work financially. After Mat decided to utilize venues that had ramp fixtures already in place, things evolved to where there would be a mini-ramp event and a separate street event over one weekend. Flatland also came back and the BS Series became the place that allowed something for everybody again. There wasn't a title sponsor in the beginning so there was very little money around, but everybody was OK with it, and actually it took away some of the negatives that big prize money brings.

– Dennis McCoy

Putting two competitors together presented big challenges. Sid Dunofsky left the company as president and was replaced by Chuck Wilke. As cash became more constrained, the resources were diverted to the two main brands, Raleigh and Nishiki; and then our parts and accessories brand, Cycle Pro. Last in line was this relatively small Southern California 20-inch brand called Haro Designs. This is where I got to know Bob, Jim, Dean, and Brad. When summoned, they would make the pilgrimage to the corporate offices in Kent, Washington. Most of us on the Raleigh/Nishiki side were jealous of this free-spirited renegade bunch that seemed to have an unfair amount of SoCal freedom and autonomy, while we were subject to all the finer elements of a Northwest pressure cooker.

– Joe Hawk

begun to shake riders from paid contracts as early as 1989; those who had once earned significant salaries now found themselves either without an income, or riding in low level shows at schools and state fairs. Haro's freestyle team was down to its bare bones. Star rider Mat Hoffman had retained a deal to ride and promote the brand through magazine presence and occasional contest entries, but his ambition to create his own products along with his efforts to resurrect interest in freestyle had caused him to leave Haro in 1991. A group of talented, new young riders including Danny Meng, Jon Peacy, Kurt Schmidt, and Bill Nitschke helped to promote Haro during the sport's leaner years through contests, magazine coverage, and occasional low-key tours. A local team that included ex-Hutch rider Chris Potts continued to fly the flag for Haro on the West Coast, albeit on a "pay-and-ride" arrangement.

As the riders' lifestyles changed to cope with these changes in fortune, the remains of the national contest scene began to stir and evolve into a format that directly reflected the vision and beliefs of the riders alone. The arrival of Mat Hoffman's Bicycle Stunt Series in early 1992 heralded a return to the multi-discipline freestyle-event format, the first since the demise of the AFA Masters series in 1989. The opening round, held at the Jeff Phillips' Skate Park in Dallas, Texas in January of 1992, was the first of six individual rounds that reached to the furthest points of the country that year. These events quickly became the mainstay and fabric of the sport's future evolution, as the riders continued to attract large crowds and forge a new direction without the burden of industry interference.

Danny Meng embarked on a short Half-Pipe tour with Mat Hoffman in 1990. Meng rides a prototype Bashguard frame.

In late 1992, having enjoyed the best and survived the worst of the larger corporate bicycle industry, Haro President Jim Ford made a decision that was poised to make or break the brand. The company's rapid mid-to-late-decade growth had resulted in the allocation of manufacturing resources to a group of Asian factories. Ties with Anlen and Anlun had been severed in late 1988, however, over capacity issues and the Wong brothers' wider interests in the bicycle industry. The search for a new manufacturing partner first led to the Alpine factory in Taiwan, via a recommendation from a senior Derby executive, but this arrangement ended quickly when Alpine went bankrupt while producing samples. An 18-month manufacturing period at the Southern Cross factory in Taiwan began in 1989 but soon ended due to issues with the quality and output of the hardware, as well as the use of questionable raw materials. After a brief period of collaboration with Redline Engineering founder Linn Kastan, who had utilized the Tijuana-based Hooker Headers factory for prototyping and a small quantity of early 1990s race bikes, it would be the company's Taiwanese mountain bike manufacturer; Kenstone Metals, that would step in to secure Haro's future.

Danny Meng became Haro's premier Flatland rider in the early 90's.

Joe Hawk,
Haro's current COO, picks up the story:

"Finally, in an effort to simplify its business and its brands as well as generate much-needed cash, Derby sold Haro in early 1993 to a private group of investors. The deal was aided largely by the efforts of Jim Ford, who had maintained a marketing and product development office in Carlsbad after Bob's departure, when Derby owned the company. All of the company's accounting, sales, and distribution efforts had been handled within the Derby infra-structure. As a result when the company was sold, it had to develop its own infrastructure from scratch.

"Jim and Brad Lusky found a warehouse and office unit on Farnsworth Court, a mile away from the previous Faraday location in Carlsbad. There, Jim and Brad began to set up shop with a small accounting crew; a designer, Dean Bradley; and a couple of warehouseman. I joined Haro in August of 1993 and arrived in Carlsbad in early September after resigning my job of 10 years with Raleigh.

"My relationship with Jim and Brad was a huge factor in that decision, but it was actually Dean Bradley who lured me down south from my home in Seattle. Knowing it was 40 degrees and more than likely raining up there, Dean would regularly call me––knowing he would get my voice mail. His message was always the same: to remind me that it was 72 degrees in Carlsbad

that day, sunny with light and variable offshore winds, with a water temp of 68 and 3-to-4-foot surf. Then he would just hang up.

"This happened several times. It was good to feel wanted. His unique recruiting method actually worked, and I bit. My immediate role at Haro was to establish the sales force internally and exter-nally; that is, after I personally assembled my Ikea desk and bolted down to Costco to find a chair and filing cabinet to complete the package. Each Haro employee had the same ritual, though, so I wasn't special. As it turned out, like all Haro employees I quickly found myself wearing other, more unfamiliar hats as we formed up each day to try and start the company all over again."

When Bill Hawkins left, a guy named Joe Mango came in and booked the shows. He drove a Camaro and smoked endless cigarettes. He wasn't from BMX but he was a genuine character, and he kept us going. At that point, there really was no money. To make a living, you had to ride in shows on a "pay per day" basis, and that's how it was at GT and the few other remaining brands too. It was all about survival. We didn't have college degrees, some of us had graduated from high school but that was the extent of what we had to fall back on outside of BMX. But I wouldn't change it for the world. It was an amazing time in our lives, but then it suddenly just disappeared. In the early 1990s, Lee Reynolds, Ed Lenander, and myself would ride at schools, county fairs, Sea World, and the odd private event at Palm Springs. But there was really not a lot going on at all.

– Chris Potts

Haro's Chris Potts rides the Haro Air Master at the 2Hip Thrasher land King of Vert Finals in Phoenix, AZ.

THE HOFFMAN
CAR INCIDENT

By Joe Gruttola

"Hoffman pulls out of a gas station and presses down on the gas pedal like he's riding toward the quarter-pipe. He was singing and laughing with a Big Gulp in his hand. Everyone was laughing with him and then we notice a car stopped in the road up ahead, making a left turn. That car shouldn't have been stopping or turning, but it was. We were still accelerating. We all noticed and started saying 'Mat'... Mat was still singing and laughing, and then there was a simultaneous 'MAT!!!' It was way too late, though. He hit the brakes, and then we hit the car. Mat, Rick, and I, and I believe Voelker or Brett Hernandez, all ended up in the front seats, snacks and drinks included (it was the 1980s, we didn't wear seat belts). There was a moment of silence and then we braced ourselves for the GT van, which was right behind us. Luckily Hadji swerved off the road in time! The dust settled and we all ran up to the car we had hit; all I saw was the driver's feet where the front seat was supposed to be. We had hit the car so hard that the front seat came off the rails and ended up in the back...the paramedics actually opened the back door to let the driver out. Once we found out no one was injured, and that the driver had been making an illegal left turn, we were back on the road. Mat vowed to never drive again. That lasted two days."

Lee Reynolds, Joe Gruttola and Lee Reynolds head straight to Vegas on the 1989 Haro Tour of Kings.

ON THE ROAD

By Joe Gruttola

"I had 13 Haro bikes during my time on the brand and gave every one of them away during tours and shows. It didn't make the guys back at the office very happy when they received bills from bike shops because I had to build another bike before a show. These kids came out to see us and gave us the opportunity to do what we were doing. I don't regret any of it. Their need was greater than mine. Rhino and Kevin Martin took great care of us. They often made the difference between a good day and a bad one. They brought the whole show together with their vocal skills on the mic and if you messed up, they would keep the crowd on your side. Everybody had bad days, so it was always great to have these two guys keeping the energy and positivity flowing and bringing the shows together."

AIR OVER 540

By Brian Blyther

"Ron was a total straight-edge, but he was still crazier than everyone else. Our Air-Over 540 routines were pretty scary at times. On a quarter-pipe we would ride side-by-side, balls-out fast toward the ramp, and he would go higher and higher, meaning I had to clear him. It was scary. On a half-pipe it was easier because I could just pump the ramp hard and get over the top of him. But if he got a long run up, he would pedal as fast as he could and go as high as he could and I would have to somehow get over the top of him. In rehearsals for the Swatch Impact tour in San Diego, one day there must have been a breakdown in communication because he decided that he was going over me and we rarely did that. We collided around 8 feet out and Ron slammed hard and got hurt. That was when Mat came in to replace him."

Blyther" airs" over Wilkerson, on the 1988 Tour of Kings.

Ron Wilkerson and announcer Tour Nar.

CHALLENGES

By Joe Gruttola

"Turning the lights off on dark roads for as long as you could. Driving with the wipers off in the pouring rain in the wake of semi trucks. Steering for somebody when they wanted to take a nap while driving, which involved using cruise control and changing lanes. This evolved into a contest. I am pretty sure I did an hour once while Rick was driving. The female underwear collections. A competition between the 'A' and the 'B' team. Luckily for us Wilkerson had just gotten married so he was out of the game."

L - R Sean Wilkerson (Announcer), Berndt Schneider, Ron Wilkerson, Sam (from New York), Lars Dorsch, Brian Blyther, Dave Nourie. 1988 Haro Tour of Kings.

Brian Blyther, Dave Nourie and Ron Wilkerson pose at a bull ring in Spain.

THE EUROPEAN CLUB TOUR

By Brian Blyther

Due to our misunderstanding of the way that dates are written in Europe [the number of the day precedes the number of the month], in 1986 we showed up for a European tour six weeks early. We land and, weirdly, there's nobody there to pick us up. We had a credit card, so we hired a Mercedes and packed all of our stuff and bikes into the back. We called Haro back in the States and told them about the mix-up on the dates and they said 'Well, do you wanna hang out, or come home?' So we decided to stay. On one of the first days we were driving to Berlin and Ron crashed the car, which was actually too small anyway so we went to the rental car place and got this Volkswagen van with a sliding door. We had that thing for around two days, and we were at a grocery store loading up with supplies when we had another problem. I was driving in the store parking lot and there were these light poles everywhere. We swung around this corner and Dave [Nourie] opens the door to dive out and a pole ripped the door and almost the entire side of the van off. We jumped out to find the door and some of the van just laying on their side in the parking lot and Ron's saying (having already crashed the Mercedes a few days earlier) 'We are NOT turning it in, we have to keep it.' So we had to rearrange all of the stuff in the back so that nothing would fall out, and there was a bit of a draft obviously. Somebody had to stay with the van constantly so we could never go to restaurants; we had to survive on grocery-store food. When we pulled into a hotel at night there was only one way of parking it...we'd just drive straight at a wall and crash into it and grind it down as close to the wall as we could get it, so if anybody tried to break into it, they would have to jump over the roof and try to slide in. We did that for an entire month and the entire right side of that van was totally destroyed. One morning in Germany, I woke up with these gross sores on my cheek and neck. At the time there was a lot of health scares around. So Wilkerson walked straight up to me and said, 'Man, you've got AIDS.' Thankfully I went to see a doctor and he said that I had gotten food poisoning in Berlin. We went on this awesome club tour, met up with all of our friends across Europe, and had a blast. Then when we went back to Germany at the end of the tour to drop the van off at the rental place, we basically crashed into the wall and left. I never heard anything more about it. It was a memorable tour."

Dave Nourie, 1987

Ron Wilkerson on the 1988 Haro Tour of Kings.

CHERNOBYL

ACID RAIN

By Brian Blyther

"In 1986 we were in Germany…somewhere right on the coast… and we were directly in the path of the acid-rain cloud from [the nuclear reactor meltdown at] Chernobyl. We didn't know much about it; we were a bunch of young Americans in a foreign place and I don't think we even had a show for four or five days. We were at this laser show on the Rhine River and all of a sudden it starts raining. Suddenly everybody starts scattering and running, and we had no clue what was happening. People were jumping into cars, getting under building awnings and doing literally anything not to get wet. It was like 80° with a little rain and people were freaking out. We were from California, obviously, so we were like, 'What's up with that?' I remember looking right down the street and we were the only ones just walking along in the rain and everybody else was just trippin' and hiding in their yards and stuff. So we found out the next day that it was acid rain from the nuclear disaster. I remember we lived off cereal in this hotel because they couldn't get eggs or anything like that. I got checked out because I started losing my hair when I was about 20. They said it was probably genetics but it just felt like a huge coincidence to me."

The fateful "flipped" rental Van.

Ron enjoying life.

Kevin Martin poses with the Haro rig which burst into flames at the end of the 1989 Tour of Kings.

AFTER HOURS

By Rick Moliterno

"Contests seemed to get a little wild on certain nights. One night in Dothan, Alabama while we were in town for an AFA contest, Ron Wilkerson was driving a van packed with just about every prominent sponsored rider from many teams. We were going out to eat. Ron always loved to get a little wild and throw some excitement into whatever was going on. That night he did an e-brake slide on the off- ramp of the freeway that got a little out of control. The van ended up on its roof with all of us inside. No one was hurt. The van rolled so slowly that Dave Nourie actually walked around the inside following the roll, staying on his feet the whole time. That event would have had a huge hole in it talent wise had it been worse! We all walked away laughing but knowing we were fortunate."

Bill Hawkins joined the company in its earliest days. Seen here with Bob Haro at the Chen Shin Tire factory.

Bill, pictured here, with a Haro dealer out on the road.

BIG BILL

By Brian Blyther

"Bill Hawkins was the person between Haro and me – and he was awesome at managing us. He was always great on the road. He let us know how far we could take things and what we could get away with. He was the buffer between Haro and the riders. He would come out on the road and if it were a good week, he would tell us that we could take the GT team out and spend a few hundred dollars on dinner and drinks. We were conscious enough to know that if we stayed with people on tour and maybe didn't get a hotel for a few days, when we reached places like New York City, we could splurge on stuff without a backlash. Bill would even everything out for us with the office and although he was a big party guy too, he could turn that off to call Bob and Jim and let them know that everything was OK, and also let us know anything that was important while we were on the road. Bill had a great way of keeping everything in line. We really felt that his job was a lot harder than it was; Jim and Bob were pretty laid back about it though as far as I can tell. They were doing their own thing. But that was why he was so good at managing everybody."

"During the show, some kid yells out, 'Hey, someone's messing with your truck. They went thataway!' We jumped on our bikes and set off and just caught a glimpse of guys on bikes riding hard into a corner. It turns out that GT had gone onto another show a town over, plus I swear I saw blonde hair and Dyno colors. They krazy-glued our locks and wrote F*%k YOU across our windshield. As we were breaking into our van after the show, I found their keys in my pocket. We tracked them down, and we all laughed over confirming it was them."

RIVALRIES:

HARO TOUR OF KINGS

By Kevin Martin

"We ended up crossing paths with the GT Dyno team several times over the summer. Lew at Freestylin' magazine upped the rivalry by creating a scavenger hunt for us to try to outdo each other. It was a really good list; not only do I still have it at home, I also have some of the items! One of the first times we crossed paths, we were stuck in traffic and it started pouring rain. I think it was either Brett Hernandez or Gary Pollack who poured shampoo on our windshield which created enough bubbles to have a rave! That was the spark that lit a summers-long prank war to end all prank wars. That night Lee somehow stole a key to the GT van. Apparently each GT guy had a key so nobody even missed it. He showed me and I told him to wait for the right time to strike. About two weeks later we crossed paths in Chicago on the Fourth of July with them and had an awesome day off of riding, finishing with watching the fireworks over the lake. We said our goodbyes and picked the next rendezvous in another two weeks in the south somewhere. That night we went grocery shopping. We bought eggs, milk, flour, and the

The milk was poured all over the carpets; the cheese was smeared underneath the dash into all of the wiring; and the eggs were broken onto the engine block so that as the engine heated up they would add to the horror of smells already coming from the van. Oh, and the best part—my favorite part of this attack––was making a funnel and filling all the air vents with flour and putting all the AC levers on full blast. The idea was after seven-plus hours of all of that shit brewing in a van that had to be at least 120° or more, their first reaction would be to turn the van on to try to get the vents to blow some of the smell away. My GT insider later told me not only did they do just that but also when the flour covered all of their faces they turned and looked at each other (faces covered in flour mind you! I am giggling writing this at the thought of that image 25 years later!) and said: 'Let's get them!' We laughed our way to Kentucky figuring payback would eventually be coming our way. Two weeks later while announcing a show, there was an unusual pause between riders emerging into the arena...

Joe Johnson, Dennis McCoy and Rick Moliterno on deck. Haro Rampage tour 1987

"The next time we saw the GT Dyno guys, we returned their keys. But that wasn't the end of it. This time they hid a large sausage under our hood, probably thinking it would smell like rotten meat when we were driving. We parted ways with some good ol' fashioned road rage, with Rick emptying a full bottle of shampoo on their windshield. They had no choice but to pull over when they turned on their wipers and the screen exploded with suds. But back to the sausage… We were driving and something smelled good. There were no restaurants in sight and we eventually realized it was coming from under our hood. We pulled over, took it out, and I had a bite. It was cooked to perfection. We will forever credit GT/Dyno for creating the first-ever 'Carbeque'!"

- Joe Gruttola

If trucks could talk. The Haro rigs were worked hard and abused. They were home to the riders for months at a time.

"It wasn't 'til the van cornered a couple blocks away that I realized it was the GT van. Those guys drove four hours each way just to get us back, on their day off! They super-glued all our locks shut, glued the windshield wipers to the windshield, spay painted FU GT/Dyno across our entire windshield. We removed the "F" part of the message and drove around most of the summer with spray paint across the windshield and spread the lie that the GT guys were mean and we didn't know why they would do that to us."

- Kevin Martin

1986. Spike Jonze poses in a Rockville BMX tee shirt with Brian Blyther while on tour.

TAKE ME TO SCHOOL

By Brian Blyther

"Spike would come out on the road with us in the summer and basically become part of the tour. One year we drove him across the entire country on the understanding that when he got to California he was going to check out film schools for when he graduated. On days off he would go into the local high school, wherever we were that day, and take classes, hang out with the smokers. He was 15, but he didn't look that old. Big Bill was coming out for the Rockford show and he was flying into a local airport. We set Spike up with a tuxedo and a limo and he went off to collect Bill from the airport. He saw Bill and walked up and said, 'Hey, are you Big Bill?' And Bill is looking like, 'Who is this kid?' They became best friends in a matter of two hours. Those two hatched a lot of pranks and schemes when Bill came out. There was always something happening, whether it was Spike lying on the conveyor belt at a Japanese restaurant, passing by and going through the curtain into the kitchen and then coming back around again. Or Bill removing all of the laundry detergent in the aisle of a grocery store and packing Spike into the gap so he could frighten passing customers and start selling it to them. Two over-active minds at work and the freedom of the tour.

"One afternoon we are taking a rental car back to an airport in North Carolina and he says, 'I bet you can't put two wheels on the grass at over 100 miles an hour.' I said there's no way anybody could do it and it would be insane to try. But I got up to 105 and edged two wheels over the shoulder, and he grabs the e-brake and yanks it on full. We were in grass up to the top of the doors spinning through gaps in trees. He was prepared for it; it scared the crap out of me. So we eventually recovered it and arrived at the airport and he starts drawing on the seat with a marker pen, and then he yanks the e-brake again on a corner and this time we are up on two wheels. He loved all that kind of stuff. We took the car back. No issues."

WINDY OSBORN

"This is one of my most iconic images personally...not for the trick or for being super-rad, but for capturing the essence of a time in the sport with back-yard ramps and all the neighborhood kids hanging out and riding for hours and hours. The scene was still raw and original back then, even though Joe is wearing a uniform. This shot reminds me of the many underground riding spots I visited back in the day, when I would go on a shoot to discover some hot new local personality. These were regular kids dreaming of a shot in the mags, a chance to put their mark on the map in the world of freestyle, hoping to be discovered and speak their voices and let the world know that they were representing their own, small-town USA. Those were golden times, and Joe was amazing. His airs were big and monsterlike, jaw-dropping and smooth.

"This particular shoot was on a very cold day, which was never too much fun for me. However, when I happened upon an opportunity to shoot such an iconic rider as JJ, against such an earthy background as his back yard, cool pics would happen. I loved having total control in private shoots like this, where I could push the rider to his limits and really get involved in the action. Creating photos for the mags was my greatest love. I wanted readers to taste and feel the talent and crazy tricks that ignited in front of my lens. Discovering these incredible kids who set the standard in the sport, and took it to insanely new levels, was an honor. A lucky girl was I, in the right place at the right time!"

JOHN KER

"The first time I ever heard of Ron Wilkerson was probably around 1982 or so; he would have been 16 at the time. I was working at BMX Plus!, and Ron called on the phone and wanted me to come shoot photos of him. Riders didn't do that very often, so it piqued my interest. He told me he could do a no-footer on a quarter-pipe. I had never seen or heard of anybody who could do a no-footer back then, so I thought it might be worth it. Still, I was a bit skeptical.

"I forget now exactly where we met and shot those photos. I think he might have brought down his own ramp from Northern California and set it up in somebody's parking lot. I think it was about a 30-minute drive to meet him, but it was worth the trip. He exceeded my expectations by a long shot. He could do absolutely amazing no-footers; high in the air, with both legs extended out about as far as was humanly possible. It looked really cool. From then on, I would shoot with Ron any chance I got. He was a super-talented and creative rider who would invent really cool tricks that nobody else was doing. He'd later invent the Nothing and the No-Handed Fakie Air.

"I shot photos with Ron every few months after that. He had amazing skills on a bike, whether he was riding ramps or skate parks, or simply doing flatland tricks on the street. Ron was always inventing tricks and finding cool locations to shoot photos.

"This photo is a simple one. It's just Ron doing a perfect Tabletop Air on a half-pipe and looking straight into the lens. I think this is from the time I shot with him with his portable ramp set up near the beach around sunset. Since Ron was looking straight at me, the flash must have blinded him, but it didn't seem to bother him much. He could do these airs in his sleep if he wanted to. He was really good."

Ron Wilkerson,
Leucadia, California, 1987

Rich Sigur
Pleasanton, Northern California. 1985

PETER HAWKINS

"Traveling south on I-5 in Northern California, the prospect of reaching the destination town of Pleasanton left two thoughts in my mind: Why this town, and would it live up to its name? East of San Francisco and nestling in the County of Alameda, a mid-sized town incorporated in 1894, and named after a US General (albeit his name was Pleasonton). On arrival it had that mixture of modern and old wild west. The original settlement was called Alisal or El Alisal (The Sycamores), and had the notoriety of being 'the most desperate town in the West,' with frequent shoot-outs in the streets, due to the presence of many bandits who were there to rob the gold prospectors of their riches. Most famously the haunt of Joaquin Murrieta Carillo, the Mexican Robin Hood.

"This weekend was to be a shoot-out of a different kind, however, with a gathering of some of the biggest names in BMX freestyle, a competition in the WIld West, and the Haro Team out in force. Ron Wilkerson, Brian Blyther, Mark McGlynn, Dave Nourie, Dennis McCoy, others too––and Rich Sigur, the subject of my photograph here.

"Photography of BMX freestyle was seemingly split into two areas, competition and photo session, and although I do have many images of the comp (and many others), I have chosen this photograph, because, in a way, it sums up the era. I mean, Rich Sigur did not go around balancing his bike in front of Pagoda-type buildings…well, I don't think he did! At a competition you shoot what is there, capturing the moment is the cliché, but setups take time and involve the rider in the vision of the photographer.

"I was always freelance, not a magazine photographer, so not for me the bag-loads of film and finger on the motor-drive button. I simply could not afford it. So I preserved my film and took time to get the shots. And now I have the chance to say a big thank-you to Rich and all the other riders who worked on the photo-session concept, for their patience in doing so."

BRAD McDONALD

"This photo of Mat Hoffman might mark the beginning of backflips as a normal trick. Up to this point, they were either regarded as a novelty act (Jose Yanez) or completely out of reach (Mat doing them on vert). Within a year of Mat showing the world that they could be done on dirt and box jumps, the trick became commonplace. Bob Kohl would even attempt a double flip in late 1992.

"The pattern of one rider with guts and motivation blazing a trail for others to follow and extend has always been an integral part of freestyle. Just as no one wanted to risk sailing off the edge of the world before 1492, no one wanted to take a chance on breaking his neck trying a backflip if he wasn't sure it was even possible. But once a rider knows a trick can be done, the risk is reduced immeasurably.

"Given how commonplace backflips have become, it's hard to appreciate just how gnarly this was back in April 1991. Mat tried and bailed on this several times. Once, possibly from one of these attempts, I saw him in a parking lot giving himself stitches to close a gash in his leg. That

might have been taking the DIY/punk rock ethos a little too far, but that's Mat.

"For me personally, this was a critical moment. A month after this contest, I was hired as the staff photographer at Go magazine. I was 20 years old and this was my dream job. Unfortunately it was short-lived––the magazine shut down seven months later. The BMX industry was in terrible shape, but that didn't deter me or many others. I started Ride BMX magazine out of my apartment in 1992; Mat started the BS Contest series that same year; and several other rider-owned brands were spawned. We had vision, a passion for the scene, and were young and had little to lose. We also had the benefit of the trails blazed by pioneers like Bob Haro, Jim Ford, Bob Morales, Ron Wilkerson, Bob Osborn, and many more.

"RIP Sin Egelja. He's the photographer in the photo. He worked at Airwalk and was a big supporter of BMX in this era."

Crystal Cove State Park in 1988 - When I was much younger, faster and better looking. Ah youth...

28 | AFTERWORD

By Dean Bradley

Some refer to it as "happenstance." A random, chance occurrence or event…That usually unbeknownst to us at the time, alters the course of our lives FOREVER. For me, one such moment in time occurred during the winter of 1979. I had just accepted a dream position as Assistant Editor at Bicycle Motocross Action Magazine. During my first-day-obligatory-tour of Wizard Publications, by Publisher/Editor/Mastermind

Bob Osborne, we strolled back into the warehouse. Amongst the pallet racks full of magazines, T-Shirts, stickers, etc., there HE was. A mop haired teenager hunched over a draftsman table cluttered with pens, X-ACTO knives, bike parts, plastic BMX number plates and various hand drawings. HE was BMXA's staff artist, illustrator, and test rider, Bob Haro. Like his unique cartoons and illustrations for the magazine, Bob was an animated, quirky, larger-than-life, almost- cartoon-character. Instantly likeable, Bob disarmed all he encountered with his humility, charm and non-stop sense of humor. In addition to his duties at BMXA, He had recently started his own company, Haro Designs. Between creating his signature illustrations for the magazine, Bob hunched over his makeshift desk in Wizard's warehouse tirelessly hand applying large decals to his plastic, injection molded "Factory Plates" BMX number plates. A one-man-production line, Bob would then individually poly bag and staple on a header card to each plate. At that time : The Golden Age of BMX, Bob , X-ACTO knife in hand, was quietly carving out his own niche as a core BMX brand, secretly selling thousands of these plates. Then tens of thousands. Then hundreds of thousands. Fast-forward seven years. After my brief stint as Assistant Editor at Wizard, I went on to work for Plus Publications, Surfer Publications, and Hi-Torque Publications serving as editor/ photographer for BMX Plus, Skateboarder, Action Now, Motocross and Mountain Bike Action Magazines. Yes, I had been busy. But, so had Bob. In the midst of our shared over ambitious careers, we had managed to stay in touch with one another. Haro Designs was now a multi-million dollar company. Bob had hired on ex-Kryptonic Skateboard Marketing Guru Jim Ford. When the opportunity arose, I joined Jim and Bob in January 1987 as Haro's Marketing Manager. As Haro Design's business grew, so did

the battle of who would distribute Bob's wildly successful and ever-expanding product line. Bicycle Industry distribution giant West Coast Cycles won that battle and IN 1987 entered into a five-year deal becoming Haro's exclusive distributor. The one-two-death-blow of more than one runaway-successful-start-up-company is always the classic lack of capitol to keep up with rapid growth combined with poor distribution/fulfillment. Well-funded distribution powerhouse West Coast Cycle's acquisition of Haro solved those issues. However, in the process, the course of Haro Designs was altered forever. To those critics who say Bob "sold out" by ultimately relinquishing control to WCC ? That's just petty jealousy and envy talking. Bob and Jim did what was ultimately essential for the survival and continued growth of Haro as a brand. Looking back, I firmly believe, Haro Bicycles is still alive and well as a result of that decision…While many, many other truly viable and innovative parts and accessory/BMX bike brands have long since come and gone. My 10-year tenure with Haro: from 1987 to 1997 indeed saw many changes as documented in this book. The once-out-of-control early-80's BMX Market suddenly, without any apparent reason, died. Sales simply dried up. Mountain Bikes became The Hottest Selling Category in the bicycle industry. When Haro decided to pursue Mountain Bikes, did Bob once again "sell out" and abandon his BMX Roots ? No. Just as Bob and I naturally progressed from BMXers into Mountain Bikers, many thousands of others were following that same natural progression. No, "sell out" is the wrong term…Today, many start-ups simply refer to it as a "pivot"…We redirected our energies and re-charted our course to best serve the rapidly changing Bicycle Industry Landscape. It was an incredibly exciting period in The Bike Industry…the likes of which I have yet to see duplicated in my 35+ years in The Business.

Just as with any bike category that emerges and dominates sales, (like BMX once did) the development of Mountain Bikes got the FULL attention of Asia's bicycle sourcing/manufacturing community. Product development was RAPID. Mountain Bike Magazines popped up seemingly overnight to fuel the fire. People like Rock Shox' founder Paul Turner came out of other industries to jump on The Bandwagon and contribute new technologies and fresh perspectives. The Golden Age Of Mountain Biking was born...And Haro pivoted their focus and effectively became an early and successful player in that arena. From The-Outside-Looking-In, it was easy for the died-in-the-wool BMX Industry pundits and press, even Haro BMX Team Riders to feel a sense of betrayal. Haro Designs was born out of BMX. Bob Haro was The Godfather Of Freestyle BMX. Haro Mountain Bikes? Haro 700c "hybrid" bikes? Haro Beach cruisers? Haro's ill-conceived F-1 Street Bikes? Haro's once high-end Fusion line of BMX performance parts whored out as OEM parts on entry-level $149 Pseudo-BMX bikes? At the time: all easily criticized tactical moves. After all, Haro was "core"... Haro was "A Rider Owned Company" before that term was coined by legions of "garage" companies who are no longer in business today. On The-Inside-Looking-Out, the perspective was way different. During my ten years at Haro, WCC had been acquired by Derby Cycle...Worldwide Raleigh: At the time, The world's largest bike company. Then Derby eventually sold off to the current Asian owners. The outcome was the same in each case...The Haro Brand quickly became a feather-in-their-corporate-cap: Their "Boutique" Brand... "The Little BMX Brand From California." Boutique Brand or not, Jim Ford's and CFO Brad Lusky's directive from any of Haro's parent companies was always the same: Profitability: Pure and Simple. "Small, soulful company founded by undercapitalized visionary sells said soul to Corporate Devil to survive." Sound familiar? It should. It plays out EVERY single day in Corporate America. Let's be clear...Bob and Jim committed no real original sin. In hindsight...The only thing we were all guilty of? Our incredible respect for what Bob had created and our shared passion to do whatever it took to thrive, survive and "sheppard" The Haro Brand through uncertain and turbulent periods in the company's evolution. Marketing/Economics 101: When its creator solely owns a niche brand, the owner can remain unwavering and "core" and ride the unpredictable ups and downs of the limited audience for their niche. When said niche brand is owned by a corporation and consolidated into a stable of other brands, the powers that be have two choices: 1) Let the brand runs its course and serve the niche: Sales numbers and corporate profits be damned...Or 2) WHEN, not if, those niche sales flatten out or drop significantly...Require said niche brand to expand its product line to serve a much broader audience...And just hope and pray you do not lose/alienate your core audience and dilute the brand's name, reputation and equity in the process. Large corporations invariably choose #2. My experience? Before and during the "courting" period of each of the three sales of Haro, The Potential Buyers gushed about how The current Haro Team were the "experts", "the brand champions", and they would leave us alone to "do what we did best." After the sale transpired and the "honeymoon" was over, and THE very first month sales faltered, The Suits (who had never swung a leg over a bike) would become instant experts in BMX, Mountain Bikes, Whatever. I remember one such occasion when top execs took issue and challenged Bob on his choice of frame paint colors and even typestyles on the bike graphics. To watch Bob's face during that fateful conference call...I sensed IT finally hit him...He had SOLD His Company. He had SOLD His Name. And in the inevitable process, he had slowly and methodically been corporately striped of his creative freedom. I refer to that moment as "The End Of Innocence", not just for Bob Haro....But to be honest, for ALL of us in that room. However, aside from The Textbook Corporate BS...As one of the core Haro Alumni, I remain truly proud of what we accomplished during the period documented in this book. The vast talent pool of people, who worked for and with Haro, rode and raced for Haro, was second to none. Yes, we worked long hours, were required to travel far away from family, friends and loved ones for many months out of the year. Yes, we all made personal sacrifices for The Brand. We also enjoyed The Privilege of producing products that changed people's lives for the better, changed people's lives forever. We were A Team...The heart and soul of a brand that still enjoys a cult-like following by industry historians and collectors alike. Yes, Bob was/is an incredibly talented visionary who unknowingly created a monster...A Brand much, much bigger than the sum of its parts. I'd like to personally and sincerely thank Bob for inviting me along for the ride...To Jim Ford for mentoring me in The Art Of Marketing...To Brad Lusky for continually stretching The Almighty Dollar and charming top riders we otherwise couldn't afford, to ride for Haro...To Chris Allen for his vast industry knowledge, incredible sense of humor and keeping me out of jail That Night in China.... To Joe Hawk for his tireless passion and continued promotion of The Brand...And finally, last, but not least, to Dom Phipps for his labors of love in so intimately documenting the history of Haro and allowing me to share my perspective.

The Bronx, New York City, 1987 - The Haro Rampage Tour. Rick Moliterno, Dennis McCoy and Joe Johnson bring color to the urban backdrop.

By the close of 1992, the once-prosperous and dynamic freestyle scene had become an alien landscape. How and why this astonishing youth sport found hard times and almost disappeared completely during this era remains somewhat of a mystery. As the author of this book, I began the process of writing and researching this story with the personal need for answers, and midway through I realized that there would be plenty.

The contributing factors to the apparent collapse of the sport actually indicate multiple theories. An exhausted market? The rise of the mountain bike? Relentlessly evolved tricks that may have cut off entry points for the next generation of riders? Nintendo games as the new youth distraction? The arrival of the video camera? High school graduations, followed by new lives and new friends at colleges and universities in distant towns and cities? Cars and girls, music and fashion, dominated our agenda. We were a youthful generation that moved on with our lives in unison.

Sitting at my desk, task-avoiding and lazily contemplating the plight of the 1980s and early 1990s freestyle scene, I log onto the Internet and become blissfully distracted by the dusty, dirty, and characterful old bikes, uniforms, and number plates that have emerged from attics, thrift stores, scrap piles, and parents' sheds, to fall back into our hands. As kids, our lives revolved around these amazing inventions: they helped to define us and we have reconnected to them in modern times through the power of nostalgia and the media. It's during such moments that I realize freestyle never died; it just completed its first cycle and the torch was passed to the next generation.

The evidence to support this theory can be seen in every neighborhood and skate park in every town and city around the world. Kids innovating on their bikes, dreaming and feeding off of each others' vision for the next breakthrough, while bravely pushing the curve further into the unknown. Unburdened by the lure of money and liberated by the freedom of a simple bicycle. Bonded and connected for life by the unrelenting brotherhood of BMX.

There are a thousand people to thank and hundreds more to celebrate as we look back. This new industry lured young entrepreneurs and creative minds to the cause, and we allowed them to build us an engine room. Riders with no agenda other than to find new ways to translate bike-riding into a lifestyle are surely the reason we saw BMX burn with the intensity of a supernova in those formative years. The photographers and writers who lived behind the glass of a camera lens or the bulk of an editor's table became our messengers; they energized and bonded us with a new language. And amongst the challenges of a new industry, the tours and police chases, sheets of plywood, record- breaking years of business, neon colors and inconceivable tricks, Haro Designs endured––a constantly evolving entity that survived the best and worst of times, standing fast to remain a leader and a force in the sport of BMX.

So whatever you believe, or whether you even care, don't delay: get on your bike and ride like it's your last day on earth.

Dom Phipps
Summer 2014

30 | THANKS AND ACKNOWLEDGEMENTS

In the process of telling this great story, a number of good people reached back into their personal archives in a bid to locate unseen and insightful imagery from the era. I would like to offer my sincere, personal thanks to the following image contributors.

Bill Hawkins, Mark Noble, John Kerr and Hi Torque Publications, Dean Bradley, Brad McDonald, Pete Hawkins, James Cassimus, Ron Wilkerson, Brian Blyther, Rick Moliterno, Tara and Barbara Llanes, Sonny and Jenny Krackau, Dennis McCoy, John Yull, Dale Matson, Jason Eley, Jeff Cousineau, John Buultjens, Joe Alder, Jeremy Alder, Kevin Martin, Jim Gray, Martin Willners, David Frame, Arnaud Pladys, Amelia Somsois, Seb Ronjon, Gork (USA BMX), Joe Johnson, Scott Moroney, Bill Curtin, Windy Osborn, John Pullman, Joe Gruttola, Matt Sully, Jay Hakala, Beccapic and Scotty Ewing. The author provided all other imagery.

The following people contributed to this project through their personal recollection of the era, through published or printed materials or through the telling, and recording of some great old stories.

The late Howie Cohen (RIP), Kay Cohen, Eben Krackau, Ron Wilkerson, John Yull, Brian Blyther, Billy Griggs, Bob Hadley, Dave Nourie, Jim Ford, Bob Haro, Pete Hawkins, Bill Hawkins, Ron Haro, Dean Bradley, Joe Hawk, Rick Moliterno, Jeremy Alder, Joe Alder, James Alder, Larry Cambra, Jess Dyrenforth, Dan Milwee, Mike King, Joe Johnson, Paul DeLaiarro, Kevin Martin, Dennis McCoy, Tara Llanes, Dale Matson, Lee Reynolds, Chris Potts, Jim Gray, Xavier Mendez, Scott Moroney, Amelia and Jean Somsois, David Frame, Brad McDonald, Danny Meng and Shawn C Jordan.

Kudos to some great online Resources – 23mag. com – memories of BMX and Johnny Ringo's Oldschoolmags.com.

My personal thanks go out to my good friend Eben Krackau and his family.

Art Direction and design; Rob White and Dom Phipps

Title: Haro Bikes – The Rise of BMX Freestyle – Volume 2 – 1987 – 1993.
Author: Dominic Phipps
ISBN: 978-0-9886035-1-6

ABOUT THE AUTHOR

Dom Phipps is a freelance writer, researcher, project manager and life long bicycle fanatic. In recent years, Dom has devised and undertaken a number of successful bicycle history projects on behalf of Haro bikes, including this series of brand history books. A native Englishman, Dom lives, works and rides in San Diego, Southern California.

www.linkedin.com/in/domphipps/